SIXTH EDITION

Tennis, Anyone?

Dick Gould
Tennis Coach, Stanford University

MAYFIELD PUBLISHING COMPANY
Mountain View, California
London • Toronto

Library of Congress Cataloging-in-Publication Data
Gould, Dick.
     Tennis, anyone? / Dick Gould. — 6th ed.
        p.   cm.
     ISBN 0-7674-1163-3
     1. Tennis.   I. Title.
GV995.G68   1999
796.342—dc21   99-27836
                                                                                 CIP

Manufactured in the United States of America

10 9 8 7 6 5 4

Mayfield Publishing Company
1280 Villa Street
Mountain View, California 94041

Sponsoring editor, *Michele Sordi*; production editor, *Melissa Williams Kreischer*; copyeditor,
Darlene Bledsoe; design manager, *Jean Mailander*; cover designer, *Susan Newman*; art editor,
Amy Folden; illustrator, *Anne Eldredge*; photographer, *Rod Searcey*; cover photo © Dennis
O'Clair/Tony Stone. The text was set in 10/12 Goudy by Thompson Type and printed on
50# Finch Opaque by Malloy Lithographing, Inc.

CONTENTS

CHAPTER 3 Playing the Game 29

PREFACE

TENNIS—what an exciting, challenging, and wonderful game! It can be played by almost anyone at almost any skill level, and the rules are the same the world over. Tennis can be the most demanding sport, or it can be played purely as a social diversion. It is a great spectator sport as well.

Tennis emphasizes values such as fair play, sportsmanship, and respect for fellow competitors. The planning and decision-making process involved in shot selection and game strategy, the maturation gained by being responsible for your successes and failures, and the participation in a recreational/competitive lifetime sport that enhances your physical fitness are significant in the general scheme of the educational process.

The "feel" of a well-hit ball on the racket or the satisfaction gained from hitting a solid shot or playing a good point is unsurpassed. Tennis is not only fun to play, but is also fun to practice and fun to learn. **The better player you become, the better you will want to be.**

Tennis, Anyone? represents a simple, no-nonsense, step-by-step approach to learning to play this great and valuable game. Its tremendous popularity as one of the best-selling "how-to-do-it" tennis instructional books ever is because it really works. I use the book "verbatim" in my physical education classes for beginners through advanced players. I also use it extensively in my methods courses and in my teacher-training programs. Many outstanding teaching professionals have begun their teaching careers with *Tennis, Anyone?* as their bible. The teaching techniques and learning progressions presented are easily applied to group situations and have been the basis for many successful and popular camp and community programs. The drills, training programs, and tactics for the more advanced players are the same as I use with my championship teams at Stanford University.

Tennis has changed remarkably during the 34 years since the first edition of *Tennis, Anyone?* Dramatic improvements in equipment, a much more scientific approach to conditioning and training methods, the structure of tennis tournaments, evolution of rules and scoring, and even the theories of how best to hit the ball have certainly illustrated that tennis is anything but a static game.

The sixth edition of *Tennis, Anyone?* has been updated. The more attractive format is simpler and easier to use, while being more fun than ever. In summary, I truly believe that whether you are a beginning tennis player, a good competitive player, or a teacher of tennis at any level, you will benefit greatly from this new edition. Most important, I hope it helps you enjoy tennis even more.

Special thanks to Chip Moreland and Vintage Contractors, and Lee De Young and Wilson Sporting Goods Company for their help with the section of the book pertaining to tennis courts and equipment respectively. And of course, my wife, Anne—also an avid player and successful teacher and championship coach—as well as my children, who have so patiently granted me the support and time to produce the various editions and revisions to *Tennis, Anyone?*

Good luck and have fun!

Dick Gould
Men's Tennis Coach
Stanford University

PART 1

The Beginning Tennis Player

CHAPTER 1

The Background of Tennis

HISTORY

Tennis has a rich and intriguing background. Its history has been marred by misfortune, but even kings could not prevent its rise in popularity. The evolution of modern tennis equipment, facilities, and methods has made tennis one of the world's most interesting sports.

Tennis is thought to be derived from a game similar to handball that was played in ancient Greece, Italy, Egypt, Persia, and Arabia. A wandering minstrel may have introduced the game to Europe by way of the ladies and noblemen of the French court. Indoors, the game was played with a rope stretched across the room serving as a net; outdoors, it was played across a mound of dirt. At first, the open hand was used to bat back and forth a cloth bag stuffed with hair. Later, a wood paddle was used.

In the tenth century, although Louis IV had banned tennis as undignified, the game continued to grow in popularity. In the 1300s, it was again outlawed, this time because Louis X believed that "tennis should be thought of as a Sport for Kings only." In thirteenth- and fourteenth-century France, tennis was known as *jeu de paume* or "sport of the hands." Its current name may be derived from the French word *tenez*, meaning "take it" or "play."

In the fourteenth century the game moved to England, but there too it had a dubious beginning—outlawed because the king felt his soldiers were wasting time playing tennis that could have been better spent practicing archery.

For the next two hundred years tennis was played very little. Interest slowly revived in France, England, and other European countries in the sixteenth century. A net replaced the rope, and a racket shaped like a snowshoe with strings was developed. Tennis became a more competitive game, and it was common to wager on the outcome of matches.

Edicts banning tennis were published, this time because of the wagering, and the sport again declined in popularity. By the nineteenth century, only the wealthy were playing the game.

The modern history of tennis began in 1873, when Major Walter Wingfield introduced lawn tennis in England. His was a fifteen-point game in which only the server could score. Called *spharistike* after the Greek root for "ball," it was played on an hourglass-shaped court divided by a net 5 feet high.

Mary Outerbridge introduced tennis to the United States in 1874. A Bermuda vacation gave her the opportunity to see British soldiers playing spharistike, and, in spite of initial difficulty with U.S. customs officials, she succeeded in bringing rackets, a ball, and a net into this country. She was largely responsible for establishing the first court in the United States—on the lawn of the Staten Island Cricket and Baseball Club. The sport caught on quickly and developed into a vigorous, fast-moving game of skill.

No one seems to know how the current scoring system evolved, although it is thought that the term "love" probably comes from the French word *l'oeuf,* meaning "the egg" or "zero." There is one theory, however: Early in France, the most common silver piece was worth 60 sous, and each of its four parts was worth 15 sous. Tennis was played for stakes, so points were worth 15, 30, or 45 sous. Eventually, after the coin denominations were no longer significant, 45 was shortened to 40 because it was easier to say.

In recent years variations of the basic scoring system have been tried. These range from "sudden death" proposals such as **VASSS,** which eliminated **deuce** games (**no ad**) and installed a "best of nine-points" tie break at six-games all, to the currently accepted twelve-point tie break. The **Point Penalty System** has been devised to help ensure fair play and sportsmanship. In addition, **The Code** now supplements the rules of tennis with explicit understandings regarding gamesmanship and etiquette. The Code includes emphasis on the basic tenet that if you are in any way unsure as to whether the ball is "good" on your side of the net, you must play the ball as good and say nothing.

In 1881, the United States Lawn Tennis Association was founded to standardize rules pertaining to scoring, equipment, and court dimensions. This organization is now called the United States Tennis Association (USTA) and follows rules and regulations set forth by the International Tennis Federation.

The USTA assists in the coordination of competitions within the United States or within countries to which the United States sends teams. The competitions range from professional events, such as the U.S. Open, to the Olympics, the Davis Cup, the Federation Cup, and all age-group competition, such as junior and senior tennis. The Open Tennis Era began in 1968 by including amateurs and professionals in the same competitive event at the same time. The men's and women's Grand Prix circuit of international yearlong events evolved in 1969. The USTA also provides a tremendous resource for the promotion and advancement of tennis in the United States. The **National Tennis Rating System** was devised to aid in defining playing abilities. This has been especially helpful in classifying players in the many recreational playing leagues.

Today, individual players, schools, recreation departments, cities, and clubs belong to the USTA. The popularity of tennis as a great spectator sport and, even more, as a lifetime participation sport continues to increase.

Important Dates in the Modern History of Tennis

1874   Major Walter Wingfield patents a set of equipment, scoring, and instructions for court layout (originally played on croquet areas)

1877   Wingfield's patent expires; new rules reestablish the court size and scoring used today; All England Championship at Wimbledon (men only)

1879   Men's doubles first played at Wimbledon

1881   United States Lawn Tennis Association established; U.S. championships initiated (men's singles and men's doubles)

1884   Ladies' singles added to All England Championships

1887   Ladies' singles added to U.S. Championships

1896   Tennis first enters Olympics and remains an Olympic sport through 1924

1900   Founding of Davis Cup, leading to international team competition for men

1913   International Lawn Tennis Association founded as the international governing body of tennis

1927   First United States Professional Championships

1963   Federation Cup competition begins, featuring international team competition for women

1968   Open Tennis inaugurated at Wimbledon (professionals and amateurs play first tournament together; only professionals qualify for prize money)

1973   Billie Jean King defeats Bobby Riggs before 30,472 people in the Houston Astrodome—a major impact in furthering women's sports and tennis in general

1988   Tennis is reinstated into the Olympic Games

EQUIPMENT

Rackets

Space-age technology has played an ever-increasing role in the evolution of tennis rackets. For decades, wood rackets were the standard. Wood **frames** featured laminations, or strips of hardwood such as maple or ash glued together to produce a strong racket. Racket size rarely varied from 27 inches long and 9 inches at the widest part. The hitting surface was approximately 60-plus square inches. The racket was described as light, medium, or heavy depending upon whether it weighed nearer 12 or 14 ounces.

However, in the late 1960s and early 1970s there began dramatic changes in the manufacturing of rackets. Metal rackets made of steel or aluminum were introduced. The word **composite** (composed of two or more space-age materials) became common as wood frames were strengthened by the addition of fiberglass and **graphite.** By the mid-1970s, the size of the racket **head** began to increase, affording the player a large "**sweet spot**"—the optimal hitting area of the racket **face,** providing best power, consistent control, and least shock and vibration. In the 1980s, terms such as **conventional** (less than 90 square inches), **midsize** (90–100 square inches), and **oversize** (100 square inches or more) were used to describe the varying hitting surfaces of racket heads.

By the 1990s, almost all rackets were either midsize or oversize. Wood frames became essentially obsolete, and most rackets were made of fiberglass, graphite, ceramic, **Kevlar, boron,** Twaron, **titanium,** or a composite of these materials. (Aluminum is still used effectively in some beginner-type frames.) The **wide-body** frame (thicker and larger) was introduced and immediately offered a much lighter (less than 9 ounces) and stiffer racket. Grip size preferences have changed over the years, decreasing from a range of 4½–4¾ inches to one of commonly 4⅜–4⅝ inches.

Factors Influencing Which Racket to Buy. Price is obviously a factor, since the cost of a new racket can approach $300. However, there are excellent frames today in the $100 range, and a beginner can do well for half that amount. (A beginner probably should tend toward a lighter, oversize frame.) The grip size, as measured by the circumference of the handle in ⅛-inch increments, may range from less than 4 inches (a very small hand, such as that of a young child) to more than 4⅝ inches (an adult's large hand). A very general rule is that the end of your thumb should be able to touch the first joint of your middle finger when holding the racket with an **Eastern forehand grip.**

MIDSIZE AND OVERSIZE

WIDE-BODY AND STANDARD

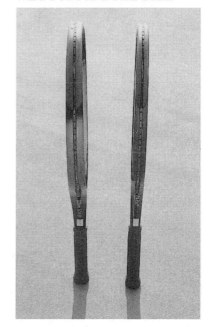

HINT: If a player has a sore elbow or arm, shock and vibration that aggravate the injury can be limited with a heavier (lead tape may be applied to the racket head) and moderately flexible racket, with a bigger grip, and strung at a lower string tension.

Personal preference is still the most significant factor in choosing the right handle size, racket weight, racket stiffness, frame head size, and racket composition. Before spending a lot of money on a racket, be certain to try out several different styles and sizes. Most large sporting goods stores and tennis specialty shops provide "loaner" rackets for trial use.

A more experienced player may let the following factors affect the choice of racket:

1. If control is more important than power (e.g., the player already hits the ball hard), a thinner wide-body that is more flexible and strung with greater string tension may be in order.

2. If the premium is on power (e.g., the player already has good control), a thicker and stiffer oversize wide-body strung with less string tension might be considered.

3. A player more comfortable playing at the baseline may want a heavier racket. If more power is the aim, the racket will probably be an oversize frame. If the premium is on consistency, a midsize racket may be tried.

4. A player who likes to serve and volley places a premium on racket maneuverability, and thus may prefer a lightweight oversize racket.

5. An all-court player, one who incorporates net attack with baseline play, may consider a frame of moderate stiffness and weight and good maneuverability for a blend of power and control.

Strings

Many "prestrung" rackets are available at department stores and large sporting-goods dealers, usually employing relatively inexpensive nylon string. Better racket frames are rarely prestrung; the buyer is able to select both the type and the tension of the strings.

String tension can vary greatly among the different sizes of racket heads. Generally, the larger the head, the greater is the string tension. You should ask the store "stringer" for suggestions as to type and tension of strings for a particular racket frame, whether it be to string a new racket, to repair a string, or to completely replace the strings in a used racket. (Strings usually lose some tension after time in the racket.) In general, use a looser string tension for more power or if you have a chronically sore elbow. However, many players advocate a tighter string tension for added control. The *gauge* (thickness) of the string may also be optional to the buyer. Better players seem to prefer a thinner gauge—which provides more "feel"—but a thicker gauge lasts longer.

There are three different types of string—nylon, animal gut, and synthetic gut. Each type has different qualities, and so the types vary in price.

Nylon is the least expensive string, starting around $15, including the cost of installation. It is moisture resistant, but top players don't think it provides the same "feel" of the ball meeting the strings as does gut in conventional or midsize rackets.

Natural-fiber animal **gut** is much more expensive than nylon, with prices starting around $30. It consists of around fifteen strands of animal intestine fibers twisted together. Oversize racket frames greatly reduce the life of gut strings because with them there tends to be more string movement and thus more wear. Also, gut can swell and deteriorate when exposed to moisture. It is, however, the preferred string of top players using midsize frames.

Manufacturers, spurred on by the need to have a string better suited to oversize racket frames and one that is much less expensive than gut, have worked hard to develop a superior nylon string. The result is **synthetic gut,** which is made of numerous nylon fibers twisted together in a process similar to that used in making natural gut. This refined process and the development of new materials give the nylon string added strength, so it is less subject to breakage or loss of tension in the racket frame. Synthetic gut costs more than monofilament nylon yet generally much less than animal gut. Studies have shown that most players of up to 4.0 (see Appendix A, page 103, for explanation of the rating system) in ability ratings notice no playability difference between synthetic gut and gut.

Balls

Tennis balls are made of rubber molded into two cups that are cemented together and covered with wool felt. Some balls are covered with extra felt for increased wear and are called *extra-duty balls*. Extra-duty balls are best on courts without too rough a surface (which causes the balls to fluff up) and at higher altitudes. The best balls are inflated with compressed air, which gives them their resiliency. Some balls derive at least part of their resiliency from rubber. Colored balls, especially yellow ones, are popular for their greater visibility compared to the formerly standard white ball.

Specifications. The official tennis ball, as defined by the International Tennis Federation, is approximately 2½ inches in diameter, weighs 2 ounces, and should bounce approximately 55 inches when dropped from a height of 100 inches.

Care. The container in which tennis balls are packed should not be opened until ready for use, since it is pressure-sealed to help retain pressure inside the ball. Commercial "compressor" cans are available to help pump pressure back into "dead" balls. Since the felt covering of a good ball will wear down, thus making the ball considerably lighter after two or three hard sets, balls are changed every eleven games or so in championship tournaments.

Dress

Until recently, the traditional tennis dress was all white, partly because white reflects heat better than do other colors. However, tennis fashion is now a thriving business, and colors and coordinated outfits are commonplace. Men wear shorts, shirt (always), socks, tennis shoes (*not* running shoes, which tend to mark the court and often have flared heels that can bring stress to knees and ankles by restricting easy lateral movement), sweater or jacket or warm-up suit, and perhaps a cap and a wrist band (moisture absorbent, to help keep perspiration from eyes and hands). Women dress the same as men, except that some women favor either a tennis dress or a skirt and top.

Shoes

Technological advances in the design and production of tennis shoes have been rapid in recent years. Gone are the days of choosing from a small selection of canvas shoes. Most major manufacturers now offer not only "low cuts," but also "three-quarter tops" (which are a little heavier but afford more ankle stability) designed specifically for tennis. These are mostly leather on the upper portion, although many styles incorporate a mesh into the design. There are sole treads designed specifically for use on hard courts, some are designed for clay court play, and some even for play on grass. This highly competitive market offers some shoes known as "cross-trainers," which can be used effectively for several different sports. The top shoes retail from $60 to over $100.

The most important factor in selecting a pair of shoes is your personal comfort in the price range you are willing to pay. Shoes of the same length size may vary significantly in width from model to model, and some feet simply fit different shoe models better than others. Durability of the shoe sole is important, as are stability, cushioning, and the flexibility afforded the forefoot. The development of **orthotics** has been a boon to people with structural abnormalities of the feet (ranging from muscular imbalance to flat feet or higher arches, bunions, and calluses) or even knee or back pain. A podiatrist makes a plaster impression of your feet and then produces a lightweight foot pad that is placed in the sole of your shoe to add needed balance and support.

TENNIS COURTS

Tennis court composition is largely determined by the climate and the tradition of a particular locale. The court can be indoors or outdoors. Outdoor courts are often surrounded by fence backdrops of polypropylene open-mesh fabric, plastic "saran," or a natural hedge. Such fencing reduces wind and increases the visibility of the ball. Indoor courts have made tennis a year-round activity worldwide. Rented court time has made indoor centers commercially attractive. Indoor tournaments, a major part of the regular professional circuit, are often played in large general-purpose arenas on a carpet-type surface.

Hard Courts

Court surfaces composed of asphalt or cement are classified as hard courts. It is the most common surface worldwide, and approximately 75 percent of the courts in the United States are hard courts. A topping is usually applied to finish the playing surface, and the texture of this finish dictates the "speed" of the court. On a "fast" court (one having a relatively smooth finish), the ball rebounds quickly and doesn't bounce as high as on a "slower" (rough) court. In general, hard courts are considered medium-fast and dictate an aggressive style of play. Two of the four Grand Slam events are played on hard courts with resilient underlayments—the U.S. Open Championships and the Australian Open Championships.

An advantage of hard courts is that the ball bounces uniformly. In addition, a minimum of upkeep is required. However, most hard courts are "resurfaced" a minimum of every four to six years in order to keep them from getting too slick and thus too slippery and too fast. Hard courts are usually colored to facilitate ball visibility, often in two tones such as light green outside and dark green inside the boundary lines. Some people feel that hard courts play too "fast," and others feel that the courts are too unforgiving on the player's feet and legs. Resurfacing is needed not only to help control the speed of the court but also to fill cracks that occur as the earth beneath the court shifts. A significant number of hard courts are being built with a resilient base. This surface tends to "cushion" the court and make it "softer" on the feet and the legs.

Soft Courts (Clay)

About 15 percent of the courts in the United States are soft courts. In many areas of the world (e.g., several European countries) the standard court is clay. In the simplest form, a soft court is constructed of well-packed and rolled dirt, with sand-like granules on the surface. The size of the granules of cinder, crushed brick, and the like largely determines whether the court is a slow court (larger granules) or a fast court (smaller granules). In general, soft or clay courts are recognized as the slowest of court surfaces. The only Grand Slam event played on clay is the French Open.

Soft courts are much easier on the feet than are hard courts. The style of play is much more deliberate, and less emphasis is placed on attack. Since the ball bounces higher and more slowly from the coarse surface, opponents have more time to get to the ball and to prepare for the return shot. A large backswing and exaggerated topspin are the norm on soft courts. Patience in setting up the point is essential, because a weak attacking shot can be more easily returned for a winner. Footing is less precise, and the player will slide more into the shot. A clay court is difficult to keep in top playing condition. It must be kept moist (watered) and be pressure-rolled at least daily, and the boundary lines must be taped, swept, or re-chalked.

Miscellaneous Court Surfaces

About 10 percent of the courts worldwide are included in this category. Grass courts have played a big part in tennis history. In fact, the United States Tennis Association was known as the United States Lawn Tennis Association during most of its existence. Wimbledon is the only Grand Slam event still contested on grass, although for decades the U.S. Open and the Australian Open were played on grass.

Synthetic grass is popular in some regions, especially in Australia. Synthetic grass requires substantially less maintenance than real grass. Both surfaces are considered fast. The ball tends to stay low and bounce, or almost skid, quickly. This leads to an aggressive style of play with an emphasis on getting to the net. (This is especially true on real grass, where the turf wears down quickly and creates many unreliable bounces.) Underspin is used extensively on grass to help keep the ball even lower, and more compact strokes are the norm.

Tennis can really be placed on any essentially smooth and rather compact surface, so the variety of surfaces is almost endless. These may be natural surfaces or artificial ones such as various carpets.

TENNIS COURT DIMENSIONS AND TERMS

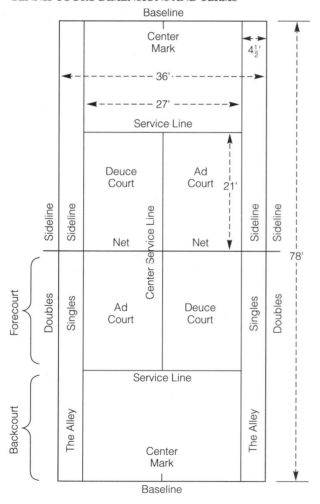

THE NET

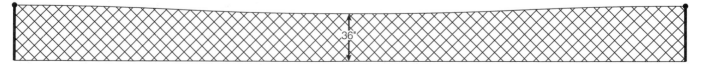

CHAPTER 2 The Basic Strokes

BECOMING YOUR OWN TEACHER

The success of *Tennis, Anyone?* is based on its ability to help you become your own teacher. To achieve this, *mental imagery* is essential. You must have a clear picture in your mind of what you want to do; at each stage of execution, you must know whether or not you have done it.

To learn the basic strokes, separate the swing into successive key parts:

1. Set Position (where to start the stroke)
2. Backswing (preparation for the shot)
3. Forward Swing (contact with the ball)
4. Finish (completion of the stroke)

You must be able to *visualize* the four key parts of the swing. This book presents "picture words" in **bold italics,** to provide mental and verbal cues to the progressions of the strokes. The text and photographs make it easy to identify key components of each part of the swing. Common faults of the basic strokes are listed for each stage of the stroke. These help you to identify correctable errors in your swing.

However, the real key to becoming your own teacher is to form a *habit pattern* by practice repetition of the correct swing. A task tends to become second nature when it is repeated again and again, whether it be walking down the street, eating with a fork, or hitting a forehand. People learn to react in an almost instinctive fashion to specific stimuli, and habit patterns are rarely forgotten.

The proper habit pattern for tennis is formed by *correcting* your swing each time you hit the ball. The start and the finish are the most important parts of the stroke. You must start and finish each swing correctly. If you have not done so, make the proper correction immediately—*before* the next ball is hit. At the finish, you can **hold** ("freeze") and check and **correct** what actually happened relative to your mental image of what you should be doing. If you start and finish the swing correctly, what happens during the swing will probably be correct as well. (The main variable is the firmness of the wrist on contact with the ball.)

The *hold and correct* phase of the stroke is the greatest factor in determining your rate of learning. It is truly the key to your initial progress.

Practice improves skill. To practice groundstrokes and volleys, start out by slowly returning balls tossed by a partner. You will have as much time as needed to **hold and correct** before having to prepare for the next shot. As the stroke becomes more second nature, return more balls more often, since there should be little or nothing to correct. Then move into a controlled practice rally and, finally, into a regular rally. By practicing the same corrected swing again and again, the proper habit pattern is quickly formed.

This book presents the basic strokes in their simplest, biomechanically efficient forms. Efficiency is important, because the more unnecessary movements you make, the greater the chance for error. Most movements in tennis should be natural movements—the difficult thing is to let them be natural. As you repeat the swing over and over and the habit pattern is gradually formed, you will relax more, and the swing will begin to "flow." The result will be a comfortable rhythm.

However, no matter how simple the stroke is initially, you cannot think of everything at once. Thus, as you **hold** your finish, focus first on **feet.** Once the position of your feet is corrected, then correct your **balance** (*body position*). Finally, when you have good balance, correct the **racket** position. The order of corrections is critical because it is impossible for the racket to finish in the right place if you are off balance. Conversely, good body balance will not be attained without proper footwork.

The concepts outlined above will now be applied to hitting the ball, beginning with the basic forehand and backhand groundstrokes. *The following presentations are geared to the right-handed player. Left-handed players must reverse the terminology.*

Readiness Drills

Spend a few minutes developing a feel for the ball on the racket and becoming accustomed to watching the ball. At this point, the grip on the racket is not of primary concern. However, the wrist should be firm. Practice the following exercises:

DOWNS

1. Softly bounce the ball *down* onto the court.

    ### CHALLENGES

    How many times can you bounce the ball down in succession? 25? 50? 100? Can you continue bouncing the ball down while you walk around the court?

UPS

2. Softly bounce the ball *up* on the racket without letting it touch the court.

    ### CHALLENGES

    How many times can you bounce the ball up in succession? 20? 50? Can you continue bouncing the ball up while you walk around the court? How long?

3. Combine both of the above exercises, and alternate several *down* bounces with several *up* bounces.

    ### CHALLENGES

    If you are in a class, try some quick relay contests bouncing the ball down, bouncing the ball up, and a combination of the two.

Short Court Tennis

Ground Strokes and Net Play are presented with the ball coming from a distance of less than full court. Play on a shorter court makes it easier to control the ball and is recommended as an introductory stage for all beginners.

If the aspiring tennis players are very young (4–8 years), there is a popular version of introductory tennis called *Mr. Pee Wee*. A Mr. Pee Wee kit, which is portable and easy to assemble, includes a small net and net posts, T-shirts and caps, 21-inch lightweight rackets, and soft foam tennis balls. Two short courts can be set up on the playing area of a regular court—each Mr. Pee Wee court will be on its own side of the regular court and is set up so that play is across the standard court, alley to alley. (The small 20- by 40-foot area may be on almost any flat surface.) Participants can have essentially instant success rallying and/or playing "points." Mr. Pee Wee can be a superb readiness game. For more information, write to Wilson Racquet Sports, 8100 W. Bryn Mawr Ave., Chicago, IL 60631, or phone (800) 272-6060.

The Forehand

First, learn the forehand grip on the racket. To get this grip, hold the throat of the racket lightly in your left hand, with the racket face perpendicular to the ground—as if the racket were "standing on edge." The racket is at waist level or slightly higher, pointing to the net. If there were a camera in the heel of the racket, it would take a picture of your belt buckle.

With your right hand, grip the handle in a "shaking hands" position. (The palm of your hand should be almost perpendicular to the ground.) The V formed by the juncture of your thumb and index finger is thus squarely on the top side of the racket handle. The thumb is completely around the racket handle. Your fingers are slightly apart, with the index finger serving as a "trigger" finger. This grip, commonly known as the Eastern forehand grip, permits you to contact the ball with the racket face acting as the palm of your hand.

Face the net and stand a little behind the T formed by the juncture of the baseline and the center mark. You may use this T as a reference for your footwork. Place your feet about shoulder width apart, with your weight evenly distributed on the balls of your feet, and with your knees slightly bent.

Move a few inches to the left of the T. From the set position, *turn* your body sideways to the net (a full shoulder rotation) by stepping with your right foot toward the T. Your left leg is relaxed, and your left foot comes up onto the tip of the toe. The racket moves back as you turn. You are now in the ready-to-hit position.

   The racket is still at waist level, with the racket head no higher than your wrist. Your hitting arm is comfortably bent. Pretend you have a camera in the heel of your racket and are going to take a picture of where you want the ball to go.

THE GRIP

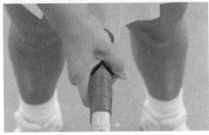

THE SET POSITION

THE BACKSWING

Common Faults

- The racket face is not perpendicular to the court ("on edge").
- The heel of the racket is not facing the belt buckle.
- The V is positioned too far to either side of the top of the handle.
- The grip is a hammer grip—that is, the fingers are too close together.
- The grip is too limp or too tight.

- The knees are too stiff.
- The body is excessively bent over from the waist.
- The racket head is too high above the wrist.
- The racket points off to the left rather than straight ahead.

- The initial step is back, away from the ball, rather than toward the T. The step is across with the left foot.
- The backswing is started after the body turn, rather than being an integral part of the turn.
- The player fails to turn completely sideways.
- The wrist drags the racket back.
- The elbow gets too far away from the body, preventing the racket from "standing on edge" and causing excessive wrist movement.
- The backswing is too high, which causes too much wasted motion.
- The racket head is above the wrist and the wrist is above the waist.
- The arm is too straight and stiff.

From the ready-to-hit position, **adjust** your feet to the ball with some quick, small steps. This helps to position your body so that your left foot may step directly toward where you want the ball to go, and enables you to transfer your weight into the direction of the shot. This final step is completed about the time the ball bounces. The left knee gives (bends) to absorb the weight transfer and to help you lower your waist to the level of the ball. With your wrist firm, contact the ball well in front of your body. Try to "carry" or "hold" the ball on the racket face as long as possible. To help you develop a feel of the ball on the racket, *hit slowly and softly.*

Always **hold** your finish until you have **corrected** the following, in order: your *feet,* your *balance,* and the *racket position.*

1. *Feet*

a. All your weight is on the front (left) foot, which is flat on the ground and at a 45-degree angle to the net.

b. The back (right) foot has only the very tip of the toe lightly touching the court, and the back leg has relaxed into a comfortble stance.

c. An imaginary straight line touching both toes should now extend toward where the ball is to be hit.

2. *Balance*

a. The front (left) knee is comfortably bent, but you are standing tall and erect from the waist, with your shoulders level to the court.

b. The racket swing has pulled your rear hip and shoulder around so that you are now squarely facing the net.

3. *Racket position*

a. Your wrist is at eye level and is firm. The racket face is "standing on its edge" so that the imaginary camera in the heel of the racket can take a picture of your left hip. The tip of the racket head is pointing above the top of the fence across the net.

b. The racket is pointing about 45 degrees beyond where you want the ball to go, which means you will be looking over your elbow after the ball. Your elbow is aligned in front of your chin.

THE FORWARD SWING

THE FINISH

Common Faults

- Failure to adjust the feet has prevented the weight to transfer into the direction of the shot.

- The hitting arm is too stiff.

- The ball is hit too late or the wrist is cocked back, which makes the ball go too far to the right.

- The ball is contacted too close to the body, which tends to make the racket head drop and the swing "scoop" the ball up too high.

- The wrist rolls over, which can make the ball go into the net.

- The wrist slaps at the ball, which brings the tip of the racket head through too soon. This results in too hard a hit or makes the ball go sharply to the left.

- The swing from the ready-to-hit position is down rather than up to the ball.

- The knee is stiff and the body is bent forward from the waist.

- The body opens toward the net too soon.

- *Feet*

  The front (left) heel rises off the court or the front foot turns open too much.

  The weight is transferred sideways—the step is not toward the net.

  The back (right) foot has not come up to the tip of the toe. The sole of the shoe should be facing the rear fence.

- *Balance*

  The legs are too stiff, causing the body to bend forward from the waist. (The back leg should be relaxed so that the back foot can slide up some.)

  The shoulders are not level.

  The hips are not facing the net.

- *Racket position*

  The wrist is not at eye level.

  The tip end of the racket fails to point out beyond the direction of the hit, and the racket face isn't "on edge."

- The elbow does not finish in front of the chin.

The Backhand

The backhand is very similar to the forehand in technique and learning progressions. One of the main differences is how the racket is held. Change to the backhand grip by using your left hand on the throat of the racket to guide it back from the set position (so that the camera in the heel of the racket can take a photo of your right hip). Simultaneously, with your right hand make a near quarter turn so the palm of the right hand is essentially on the top of the racket. The inside of the top knuckle of the index finger rests squarely on top of the handle. Your fingers are slightly spread, and the thumb may give added support by being diagonal or slightly angled down the back of the handle. This grip is known as the standard Eastern backhand grip, and is recommended for beginning players because it puts the racket face and wrist in position for solid ball contact.

Stand a little behind the **T** at the back of the court and face the net. Place your feet about shoulder width apart, with your weight evenly distributed on the balls of your feet, and with the knees slightly bent.

THE GRIP

THE SET POSITION

Common Faults

- The top knuckle of the index finger is not positioned on top of the handle.
- The grip is a hammer grip—that is, the fingers are too close together.
- The grip is too limp.
- The grip has not turned enough from the forehand grip.
- The thumb is straight instead of diagonal across the back of the handle.

- The knees are too stiff.
- The body is excessively bent over from the waist.
- The racket head is too high above the wrist.
- The racket points off to the left rather than straight ahead.

THE BACKSWING

Move a few inches to the right of the **T** from the set position. *Turn* by stepping with the left foot toward the **T** and come up onto the tip of your right toe. This allows you to complete a full shoulder turn. Bring your racket back the rest of the way, with your left hand still lightly holding the racket at the throat. Except for the grip, the backhand ready-to-hit position is like that of the forehand: The racket is at waist level, with the racket head no higher than the wrist, and the camera in the heel of the racket is taking a picture of where you want the ball to go. However, your hitting arm is comfortably straight and the other hand still rests lightly on the racket throat.

- The initial step is back, away from the ball, rather than toward the **T**. The step is across with the right foot.
- The backswing is started after the body turn, rather than being an integral part of the turn.
- The player fails to turn completely sideways or turns too late.
- The backswing is too high, which wastes too much motion, and the elbow is bent rather than comfortably straight.
- The left hand lets go of the racket too soon.
- The racket head is above the wrist and the wrist is above the waist.

Now that you are ready to hit, take some quick *adjusting* steps. These steps enable you to position yourself so you can transfer your weight into the direction of the shot by stepping toward the net with your right foot at about the time the ball bounces. The right knee gives (bends) to absorb the weight transfer and to help you lower your waist to the level of the ball. With your wrist firm, contact the ball well in front of your body. Hit the ball softly by lifting it out toward the net. Slowly let the tip of the racket follow out after the ball.

Always *hold* your finish until you have *corrected* the following, in order: your *feet,* your *balance,* and the *racket position.*

1. *Feet*

   a. All your weight is on your front (right) foot, which is flat on the ground and at about a 45-degree angle to the net.

   b. Your back (left) foot has only the very tip of the toe lightly touching the court, and the back leg has relaxed into a comfortable stance.

   c. An imaginary straight line touching both toes should now extend toward where the ball is to be hit.

2. *Balance*

   a. Your front (right) knee is bent comfortably, but you are standing tall and erect from the waist, with your shoulders level to the court.

   b. The racket swing has pulled your rear hip and shoulder around so that you face at a 45-degree angle to where you want the ball to go (not quite as much of a turn as with the forehand).

3. *Racket position*

   a. Your wrist is approximately at eye level and is firm. The racket face is in the same plane as your shoulders, the imaginary camera in the heel of the racket can take a picture of your front (right) hip, and the racket head is well above the wrist. The racket is almost at a 90-degree angle to the court.

   b. The racket arm has swung about 45 degrees beyond where you want the ball to go. Your left hand has lightly followed the racket at the start of the swing, so that it now rests just in front of your waist.

THE FORWARD SWING

THE FINISH

Common Faults

- Failure to adjust the feet has prevented a weight transfer into the direction of the shot.

- The ball is contacted too late, which makes the ball go to the left.

- The tip of the racket comes through too soon, which makes the ball go to the right.

- The ball is contacted too close to the body, which tends to make the elbow bend, the racket head drop, and the swing "scoop" the ball up too high.

- The left arm fails to help initiate the forward swing by not guiding the racket toward the ball.

- The elbow bends (often because the guiding left hand has released the racket too soon), which causes the racket head to rise above the wrist and brings the swing (and ball) down.

- The wrist fails to remain firm, causing the racket head to drop and making the ball go too high.

- The body opens up too much toward the net, often due to late ball contact.

- The ball is hit too hard and abruptly, rather than being smoothly lifted out into the direction of the hit.

- *Feet*

   The front (right) heel rises off the court or the front foot turns open too much.

   The weight is transferred sideways. The step is not toward the net.

   The back (left) foot has not come up to the very tip of the toe.

- *Balance*

   The legs are too stiff, which causes the body to bend forward from the waist.

   The shoulders are not level.

   The body is facing toward the net too much.

- *Racket position*

   The wrist is not approximately at eye level.

   The racket tip fails to point out beyond the direction of the shot and fails to finish above the wrist.

   The finish is not far enough around the ball to the right of the body.

The Two-Handed Backhand

THE GRIP

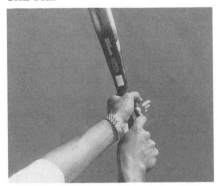

THE SET POSITION

THE BACKSWING

If you are relatively small, lack strength in your wrists, or have a sore elbow, you may have less strain on your arm if you hit the backhand with *two* hands holding on to the racket. (Many top players who use two-handed shots began doing so at an early age when they needed the extra hand to give added support to the racket.) In addition to increased strength, advantages of the two-handed backhand include a very precise stroke, heavy ball pace and penetration, and a tremendous amount of disguise to the direction of the shot.

The disadvantages of using two hands include a premium on precise footwork, possible confusion when learning to volley, and reduced flexibility for spinning the ball, especially for obtaining underspin on approach shots and on serve returns.

Try both the one-handed backhand and the two-handed backhand to see which feels best. Utilize the following techniques for hitting the two-handed backhand.

The Mechanics

The racket is held with a regular backhand grip, with the right hand at the base of the handle and the left hand higher up on the handle. Two-handed players usually use a fairly straight backswing and always make a complete pivot, since having both hands on the racket pulls the front shoulder well around toward the net.

Footwork is more critical in two-handed shots than in one-handed shots. If you are late getting to the ball and have to step to the side (parallel to the baseline) to reach it, your back side (left side of the backhand) is prevented from turning into the shot; thus you are forced to rely too much on your wrists to get the racket head through the flight of the ball. Try to position yourself to step straight into the line of the shot so that your left hand can help pull your left hip through on the finish.

On contact, try to keep the racket face on the ball for as long as possible by letting the racket tip come around the outside of the ball. To do this, keep the wrists firm, and be certain on the finish that the racket head is not turned over and that the racket and your arms are pointing in the direction of the shot. You can think of the two-handed backhand as a left-handed forehand.

THE FORWARD SWING

THE FINISH

Practicing the Forehand and Backhand

Practice with a Partner

The best way to practice hitting is with a partner who tosses the ball to you. The hitter starts at the baseline a little to the side of the T, with the tosser on the same side of the net. The tosser should toss the ball softly underhand to a spot about 10 feet in front of the hitter. The tosser should toss only when the hitter has completed the backswing and is in the ready-to-hit position. The ball should be returned softly so that the tossing partner can catch it at head level. (The ball would clear the net by 3 or 4 feet if the partner did not catch it.)

> **CHALLENGE**
>
> Practicing a *corrected* finish, how many of ten forehands can you hit that your partner can catch? How many of ten backhands?
>
> *IMPORTANT:* If your finish is not *corrected,* the shot does not count even if your partner can catch the ball. (Your partner should need only one ball if you can hit a catchable ball each shot.)

TURN; TOSS AND ADJUST

Use Adjusting Steps

Even when the tosser has a target, the ball is not always where you want it, making it difficult to transfer your weight directly into the shot. Before committing yourself to your final step into the shot, try taking some little "adjusting" steps as the ball leaves the tosser's hand. If the ball is too close, you can quickly adjust backward; if the ball is too far away, you can adjust forward and step into the hit.

Use "Picture Words" to Help Your Mental Imagery

To help you become your own teacher (or if someone else is helping you), think— or say aloud—the following words as you stroke:

STEP AND HIT

> *Turn:* Step and take the racket back to the ready-to-hit position.
> *Toss:* Signal the moment for your partner to throw the ball.
> *Adjust:* Take a couple of quick steps immediately as the ball is tossed to position your feet so you will be able to transfer your weight into the shot.
> *Step and hit:* Step onto your front foot and then hit the ball.
> *Hold:* Freeze at the end of the shot in order to see what you did.
> *Correct:* Correct your *feet, balance,* and *racket position* while holding; thus, you make the correct swing a habit.

The Importance of Holding and Correcting

Holding is important because it allows you to visualize what you have done during a swing. By *correcting* what was wrong, a habit of doing the right thing can be formed. Ask your partner to help you with your corrections. *Never* hit the next shot until you have corrected the first.

HOLD AND CORRECT

Since it is difficult to hold the racket in the correct position unless you are balanced, and almost impossible to have good balance without good footwork, *always* **hold and correct,** in order, your *feet,* your *balance,* and your *racket position.*

General Hints

You may feel restricted and stiff at first, but try to develop a soft, slow, fluid hitting motion. Think of a gradual "slow motion" swing—"catching" the ball and "holding" it on the racket, rather than "hitting at" the ball. As you get a feel for what you are doing and develop a rhythm, have your partner toss as you start to take your racket back, rather than waiting until it is all the way back in the ready-to-hit position.

Returning Wide Balls

THE WIDE FOREHAND

THE BACKSWING

THE FORWARD SWING

THE FINISH

THE WIDE BACKHAND

THE BACKSWING

THE FORWARD SWING

THE FINISH

You are beginning to feel comfortable returning balls that come close to you ("adjusting forehands and backhands"). You are gaining more control of the ball. You have little need to correct your finish, since the basic swing has become a habit.

Now you are ready to hit forehands and backhands for which you must run farther. Take a couple of recovery side skips away from the T (to the left for a forehand, to the right for a backhand). *Turn* by stepping with the foot nearer the direction you wish to go. (The first step is with the right foot for a forehand, the left foot for a backhand.) Simultaneously take the racket back to the ready-to-hit posiiton. Run smoothly to the T. Your partner will **toss** after you reach the T, if you have your weight on the correct foot (the right foot for a forehand and the left for a backhand) and if your racket is in the proper ready-to-hit position. As the ball leaves your partner's hand, **adjust** your feet to the toss before stepping into the shot. Hit and **hold** your finish to check and *correct* your *feet,* your *balance,* and the *racket position. Recover* by exchanging the position of your front foot with that of your rear foot, and sideskip back to your home base. *Remember:* Always run to the ball with your racket back in the ready-to-hit position.

Develop a Practice Rhythm

When you feel comfortable with returning wide balls, and are holding and correcting, your partner tosses as you near the T so that you never have to come to a complete stop before stepping into the hit. (*IMPORTANT:* You, the hitter, must *always* initiate the action. If the tosser tosses before you have turned and started to run, you will have to play "catch-up" with the ball, and you will probably not be able to transfer your weight correctly into the shot.) During an actual game, it is often impossible to get to the ball in time to transfer the weight into the shot. When this happens, it helps to let the rear leg relax so that the back foot can slide around and allow you to finish with your feet "in line."

You soon get the feeling of constantly moving. As soon as you have recovered, push off, turn by stepping, and go directly into your next hit. *Always* pause at the finish to make any necessary corrections. Many balls can thus be hit in succession in a short time.

CHALLENGE

How many of ten balls can you hit with a **corrected** finish that your partner can catch?

Practicing with a Ball Machine

Beginners should set the machine for a fairly slow ball and a long interval between shots. *Before* the ball is released, **turn,** take the racket back, and begin running to the spot where the ball will most likely be. (This gives you time to reach the ball without being hurried.) **Adjust** your feet while the ball is in the air, and **hold and correct** the finish before recovering back to the starting point. Try to develop a smooth rhythm on shots. Always aim to a target on the court.

CHALLENGE

Place targets (cones) in each quarter of the playing court. Hit five balls to each target area. How many consecutive balls to each successive target area can you hit? Use mostly crosscourt shots for the targets in the service court.

Returning Deep Balls and Short Balls

THE DEEP FOREHAND

To return a high, deep ball, you move back. To return a short, low ball, you run in. To practice moving back and in, use the **T** as your home base. Your partner may now alternately toss a high, deep ball that lands near the baseline, and a soft, short ball that lands near the service line.

THE SHORT BACKHAND

The Deep Ball

For the deep ball, step back as you turn (onto the right foot for the forehand, onto the left foot for the backhand). The object is to run far enough back with cross-over steps to allow the ball time to descend to waist level from the peak of its bounce before you hit. Since you are now farther back in the playing court, you must return the ball higher so it will go deep. (You will be hitting a ball that approximates a **lob,** arcing quite high above the net.)

Turn and take your racket back to a ready-to-hit position that is lower than normal. Lean slightly backward, lowering your rear shoulder. This points the heel of the racket up toward where you want the ball to clear the net, and puts the racket head slightly below your wrist to permit you to hit up to the ball.

Your partner tosses high as you start back, giving you time to adjust your feet and still be able to step into the ball. Lift the ball up so it arcs upward toward the net and "falls down" to your partner. *Hold* your finish and *correct.*

THE BACKSWING

THE BACKSWING

The Short Ball

Turn, and take the racket halfway back to the ready-to-hit position, as you move forward for a short ball. As your partner tosses short, you turn the rest of the way. Adjust your feet and step into the shot. (Since the short ball is usually a low ball, lower the racket head in the ready-to-hit position to slightly below the wrist, as you do for a deep ball.) Hit by lifting the ball up to your partner, and *hold* and *correct* the finish. Although you bend more from the knees to get the ball, you always finish standing tall from the waist. If you must take a large step to reach the ball, the rear leg must relax on the finish. This allows the rear foot to slide up to help you balance.

THE FORWARD SWING

THE FORWARD SWING

CHALLENGE

While alternating deep balls and short balls, how many of ten short balls can you hit that your partner can catch?

Use a Steeper Ball Trajectory

THE FINISH

Both the deep ball and the short ball must be returned at a higher trajectory than normal—the deep ball in order to carry it deep, the short ball in order to clear the net. Aim to contact the bottom of the ball by starting the swing not only with the racket head lower than usual but also by beveling the racket face slightly open (perpendicular to the anticipated flight of the hit ball). (The heel of the racket in the ready-to-hit position points up into the trajectory you want the ball to take above the net.)

THE FINISH

The Practice Rally

Returning only one ball at a time, as you do when a partner tosses to you, allows you as much time as you need to correct each shot. As you form habit patterns and gain confidence in your ability to correctly hit and control tossed balls, you should move into the more realistic situation of returning balls that are *hit* to you. The practice rally is presented in three learning progressions—starting the rally (one-hit rally), returning the ball (two-hit rally), and keeping the ball in play (forever rally).

The Practice Rally Position

Start with both partners just behind the service line. Standing up close rather than "full court" helps you remember to hit softly and thus gives you time to correct your finish before the ball can be returned.

Since most balls hit by beginners are forehands, the forehand rally is emphasized here. Use the alley as your target, and stand outside the alley so that the ball will be to your forehand if it lands in the alley. Or, use the service court, but stand off center so that most balls landing in the service square will be to your forehand. This allows you to prepare early and without hurry, and means you are able to take the racket back to the ready-to-hit position before your partner hits the first ball.

Starting the Rally (One-Hit Rally—Forehand "Starts")

Turn and take your racket back to the ready-to-hit position. When the racket is completely back, **toss** the ball up so it bounces in front of you toward the net. When the ball leaves your hand, quickly take a couple of **adjusting** steps to ensure that you can transfer your weight into the line of the shot. Softly hit the ball up into your partner's target area and **hold and correct** your **feet, balance,** and **racket position.** Your partner can gain valuable practice in judging the ball by taking the racket back when you do, adjusting the feet quickly to your hit, and then getting into position to step into the hit ball and catch it with the free (left) hand. If the ball comes high, the hitter learns to adjust back and let the ball drop down. If the ball comes low, the hitter learns to bend the knees in order to catch it at waist level. If the ball is to either side, the hitter gets practice by adjusting either away from or toward the ball. Play catch with your partner in this manner until you can control the speed and trajectory of the ball and always **hold and correct** the finish.

Hints for Controlling the Ball

The following hints will help you hit softly in an arc: In the ready-to-hit position, lower the racket head slightly below your wrist by lowering your back (right) shoulder. Start with your hitting arm slightly bent at the elbow and held so the imaginary camera in the heel of the racket takes a picture of where you want the ball to clear the net. Toss the ball up so it bounces high and allows you to hit it from underneath. Step forward and let your front (left) knee bend while standing tall from the waist up. Follow through completely but slowly.

To help control the direction of the hit, keep your wrist firm and try to feel the ball on the racket face as long as possible. "Push" the ball into the direction of the hit, and don't be in a hurry to follow through. Your objective is to hit the ball so it approximates a tossed ball moving in a soft arc (rather than a beeline). The ball should go up and then "fall down" into the alley, short of the service line.

CHALLENGE

How many of ten balls can you softly hit within the alley and with a corrected finish? (As an alternative, the rally may take place in the service square.)

THE PRACTICE RALLY POSITION

STARTING THE RALLY

ALTERNATIVE: SERVICE SQUARE RALLY

Returning the Ball (Two-Hit Rally)

When you and your partner can control the speed and direction of the one-hit rally (for example, regularly hitting most shots into the target area), you are ready to progress to the two-hit rally. Both you and your partner **turn** and take your rackets back to the ready-to-hit position at the same time, as in the one-hit rally. Hit the ball softly to your partner, who returns it if it lands in the target area. **Hold** your finishes and **correct,** especially to see if you have adjusted your feet to allow yourself to step into the flight of the ball. (Let the ball go by if it comes back to you.)

**TWO-HIT-RALLY POSITION
(FOREHAND TO BACKHAND)**

> **CHALLENGE**
>
> Practice until you and your partner can complete at least ten two-hit rallies with corrected finishes.

If you wish to try some backhand returns, adjust your ready-to-hit position so the ball will most likely go to your backhand. If your partner is starting the rally by hitting into the alley, you should move to the other side of the alley so the ball will be to your backhand.

The Crosscourt Two-Hit Rally

Try a crosscourt two-hit rally. Use the diagonally opposite service square as your target area and hit across the court. To prepare, emphasize turning to the ready-to-hit position so your side and shoulders are diagonal to the crosscourt service square. Toss the ball so you can adjust your feet to step diagonally toward the crosscourt target area rather than straight ahead toward the net.

CROSSCOURT RALLY

Keeping the Ball in Play (Forever Rally)

It should be an almost natural progression from the two-hit rally to "keeping the rally going." As long as you are not hurried, and as long as the ball lands in the target area (either the alley or the service square), return the ball to your partner. Try for a three-hit rally, and if you achieve it, return the ball for a fourth time, and so on. Emphasize having your racket back *before* the ball lands on your side of the net, but **hold** your finish (and **correct** if necessary) until your shot lands on the other side. (Since you are hitting almost all forehands, there is no need to come back to the set position after each shot. However, if the ball should go to your backhand, and you have the time, return it with a backhand shot.)

FULL-COURT FOREVER RALLY

> **CHALLENGES**
>
> How many balls can you keep in play with a corrected finish?
>
> Gradually move back to full court, hitting softly and with arc, and holding your corrected finish until the ball lands on the other side. (Each partner should now return to the set position after each shot.) How many balls can you keep in play with a corrected finish? How many that land beyond the service line on the forehand side of the court? The backhand side?

USING THE BACKBOARD

Rallying with the Backboard

After you have had some practice with the forever rally, a backboard may be used to advantage. The same principles apply: Don't hit too hard; and first practice only forehands, then only backhands (without returning to the set position). Hit to a target, such as a chalk mark on the wall. You may wish to let the ball bounce twice to give you more time to prepare.

The Serve

Most people who find the serve difficult fail to think of the serve in progressive steps. It is hard to throw the ball up correctly if you are already worrying about dropping the racket behind your back. It is hard to drop the racket if you are thinking ahead to contact. Thus the serve presentation is divided into two parts—(1) the backswing and ball toss and (2) the forward swing and hit.

The Backswing and Ball Toss

Start in the set position, with your left side toward the net, your weight on the back foot, a forehand grip on the handle, with your left hand cradling the throat of the racket, the racket pointing in the direction of the hit. The ball is held in the thumb and the first two fingers of the left hand.

Let both arms drop together toward your front (left) leg. Use these picture words: **Both arms down together.** Now concentrate on the toss. *HINT:* Hesitate a few times at this point so you can get your focus entirely on the weight transfer and ball toss.

Transfer your weight onto your left foot as your left arm begins to extend up for the toss and as the racket starts to travel past your toes in a wide arc toward the fence behind you. The palm of the racket hand faces down. As your left arm reaches up, release the ball. Toss the ball about 2 feet above your extended left hand and about 6 inches in front of your left toe. Use these picture words: **Now, weight forward and toss.**

To check the accuracy of your toss, let the ball drop back down into your hand. As the hitting elbow reaches shoulder level, it bends about 90 degrees, which permits the tip of the racket to be pointing straight up. In essence, the racket and hitting elbow form the letter **L**. You have now completed the backswing and ball toss and are in the ready-to-hit position. You should **hold and correct** three things: (1) The ball tossing arm is extended straight up to catch the ball, (2) your weight has transferred onto your front foot, and (3) your racket arm is in the L position.

CHALLENGE

Practice your backswing and ball toss until you can catch the ball toss in the proper ready-to-hit position five times.

THE SET POSITION

BOTH ARMS DROP DOWN TOGETHER

WEIGHT TRANSFER AND BALL TOSS

READY-TO-HIT POSITION

Common Faults

- The grip tends to a "hammer" grip rather than a forehand grip. (As you improve, you should gradually move the grip to between a forehand and a backhand.)
- The weight starts on the front foot.
- The ball is held in the palm of the hand.

- The left hand has lowered to a position beside the front leg rather than in front of it, thus preventing the arms from rising together.

- The arc of the backswing is cramped because the racket wrist turns up on the backswing, causing the elbow to bend before it reaches shoulder level.
- The backswing is not in the hitting plane. In other words, the tip of the racket head fails to point to the fence behind the hitter.
- The backswing and ball toss are hurried, probably because you are prematurely concerned with ball contact.

- Instead of bending the elbow to get the racket high enough to drop, the wrist bends back, thereby preventing a smooth, full transition from the backswing into the forward swing.
- The ball toss is too low because the left arm does not follow through high enough on the toss.
- The ball toss is too far back because either the weight didn't transfer forward on the toss, or the left hand flicked the ball instead of "placing" it in the air.
- The hitting elbow is not at shoulder level and the tossing arm is not fully extended up at the conclusion of the backswing. The racket and the arm do not form an L.

The Forward Swing

The forward swing begins from the ready-to-hit position. The racket now drops behind your back as the elbow moves forward in a "throwing motion."

Picture words for the forward swing describing the racket drop and ball contact are *drop and hit.*

The throwing motion continues as the racket arm extends upward to contact the imaginary ball and as the wrist snaps up into the hit. The tossing arm drops across the body.

Continue the follow-through out into the direction of the hit and then down to your left side.

Balance by letting the back heel come off the ground and by relaxing the back leg as the back foot turns.

Make this entire throwing motion as smooth as possible. Keep repeating this motion in two parts—(1) the backswing and ball toss and then (2) the forward swing.

Now, instead of catching the ball, continue the swing and softly hit the ball. Remember to *hold* the finish and to *balance.*

Practicing the Serve

Always practice a few backswing and ball tosses as a warm-up. Remember to catch the ball by letting it fall down into the hand of the completely outstretched left arm. Then, serve softly and slowly, while saying picture words to yourself: *Both arms down together; now, weight forward and toss; drop and hit; balance and correct.*

CHALLENGE

How many of ten balls can you serve into the proper service court? If a court is not within easy access, use a wall and draw a circle about 4 feet from the ground. Stand approximately 36 feet from the wall. How many times can you serve into the "target" on the wall?

THE RACKET DROP

THE HIT

THE FOLLOW-THROUGH

THE FINISH

Common Faults

- The racket does not drop far enough behind the back. (Think of having, or try to have, the wrist touch the shoulder before hitting the ball.)
- The racket drop is accomplished by a bend from the wrist rather than from the elbow.

- The right side turns forward too soon. (To help prevent this, let the tossing arm drop across the chest.)

- The throwing or hitting motion is cramped. (Be sure to reach up high to hit, and don't let the ball drop too low.)
- The hitting motion is down to the ball rather than up. Not enough wrist action is used.
- The hit is too hard and doesn't have enough arc, which means the body is not relaxed and the swing not loose enough. This causes the body to "muscle" the serve. (Actually try to hit the ball upward.)

- The body falls off balance, probably because the left foot does not stay anchored flat on the ground or because the back leg is still and the back foot has not turned. (Keeping the right foot back forces you to hit only good tosses, for the foot cannot step out to reach a bad toss. It also helps give you the proper rhythm of the racket-drop and shoulder-turning action up into the hit.)

Net Play

You are now ready to begin net play. Forehand and backhand volleys and the overhead are discussed. For the volleys, you and your partner should stand about 10 feet apart (on opposite sides of the net if you are on a court). Start net play in the set position, with the racket head at chest level and your arms forward so that the elbows are slightly in front of the body. The volley is divided into two parts: (1) the preparation and (2) the hit.

The Forehand Volley

To *prepare* for the forehand volley, step forward with the right foot as you push the palm of your racket hand forward (letting go of the racket with the other hand). Turn your body slightly so you face the racket squarely. You should be slightly sideways to the net, with the racket face approximately parallel to the net. The racket head is slightly above your wrist and well in front of your chest. Your hitting elbow is slightly bent in front at your right hip.

When you have prepared by "showing" the hitting face of your racket to your partner, your partner softly *tosses* underhand to the racket. For the hit, *step* toward the ball with your left foot *and "block"* the ball toward your partner's head. Keep your wrist firm. The step and elbow action provide power. Use these picture words: *prepare, toss, step and block, hold and correct.*

Hold the finish and check to see that your racket face is still almost parallel to the net and the racket head still above your wrist with the left hand in front of your left hip. (The tip end of the racket head should be slightly forward.) Your weight is all on the front foot, with the toe of the back foot lightly touching the ground. If you are returning a low ball, bend from the knees rather than from the waist.

CHALLENGE

How many of ten tossed balls can you return to your partner? *HINTS:* (1) You must "show" your racket face to your partner before the toss. (2) Slowly block the ball back so that your partner can catch it at chest level. Gradually toss the balls farther away from the hitter and mix in some lower tosses.

THE SET POSITION

THE PREPARATION

THE HIT

THE FINISH

Common Faults

- Elbows are against your side.
- The racket head is too low.

- Too much backswing is used, which causes the ball to be contacted late and not in front of the body. (Remember to prepare by keeping your elbow in front of your body.)
- The racket is too high (almost vertical to the ground), which will make low balls go into the net.

- The wrist fails to remain firm on contact, which causes the racket head to drop below the wrist on the finish.
- Don't rush your volley practice. Be certain to do the volley in two parts—(1) the preparation and (2) the hit. Your partner tosses only after the preparation has been completed.
- Don't lunge at your volleys.

- The racket head drops below the wrist after contact.
- The racket face "slaps" at the ball. It fails to remain almost parallel to the net after contact.
- You bend forward too far from the waist and not enough from the knees when returning low balls. This causes many balls to go into the net.

The Backhand Volley

Prepare for the backhand volley by pushing your right hand forward as you change grip. (This puts the racket basically parallel to the net, so the racket face is now in position to hit the ball.) At the same time, shift your weight onto your left foot and turn to face the racket squarely.

Now your partner *tosses* to the racket and you *step* onto your right foot, toward the ball. Keep your left hand still, but with your right arm push the racket forward, holding your wrist firm, to hit (or *block*) the ball back toward your partner's head. Use these picture words: *prepare, toss, step and block, hold and correct.*

Hold the finish and check to see that the racket head is still above the wrist. (The tip end of the racket head should be slightly forward.) All your weight is on the front foot, with the toe of the back foot lightly touching the ground. If you are returning a low ball, bend from the knees rather than from the waist.

Practice Against a Wall

Some value can be gained by practicing the volley against a wall. Stand 4 or 5 feet from the wall and volley the ball up against the wall. Hit *softly* and hit either forehands or backhands—*not both*. (Don't return to the set position.) This is a good way to practice footwork and to set the habit of keeping your hitting elbow and the racket in front of your body.

CHALLENGE

How many forehand volleys can you hit in succession? Backhand volleys?

THE PREPARATION

THE HIT

THE FINISH

VOLLEY PRACTICE

Common Faults

- You forget to change your grip.
- The racket does not stay away from and in front of the body.
- The left hand lets go of the racket too soon.
- The body does not turn enough.

- The ball is contacted late (too close to the body).
- The swing is not enough from the shoulder. (The forehand volley relies more on the elbow joint.)

- The racket head drops below the wrist after contact. (The wrist must remain firm.)
- You bend too far forward from the waist, rather than from the knees, which tends to make low balls go down into the net.

- The player volleys the ball down rather than slightly up, which makes it impossible for the ball to rebound from the wall back into the hitting position.
- The player swings too much and too hard. (Against a backboard there is only enough time for light hits.)
- The player fails to keep the ball to only the forehand side or only the backhand side. (Again, there is only enough time for one or the other kind of shot, but not enough time to interchange shots.)

The Overhead

For the overhead shot, your tossing partner should be about 10 feet away from you but should stand off to the side so the hit ball does *not* go back to where it was tossed. The ball should be tossed underhand so it goes high and almost straight up, which gives you time to adjust your feet to the ball. The overhead is practiced in two parts—(1) the preparation and (2) the hit. For picture words, use *prepare, toss and adjust, tap, hold and correct.*

To *prepare,* take a step back with your right foot (turning your left side toward the net). Pick your racket straight up from the set position to a position similar to the serve ready-to-hit position. (Your hitting elbow should be at shoulder level, and your arm should be bent so the racket is above your head.) Pointing your left hand up to the ball may help align your body to the ball.

When you are in the ready-to-hit position, the ball is *tossed. Adjust* your feet by sliding forward if the ball is short, or by sliding back if the ball is deep.

For the hit, transfer your weight onto the front foot and let the racket drop only a little behind your back (to the shoulder blade) as the hitting shoulder turns forward. Bring your racket forward and up to contact the ball. Use a firm snap of the wrist to hit the ball. Keep the follow-through short, almost as if *"tapping"* the ball. The left arm is tucked across the body.

Hold to see that your weight is balanced on your front foot, the back toe is turned, and your wrist is "broken," with the racket head tip pointed down and out in the direction of the hit. As the lob goes deeper, however, you may not have time to set up and step into the overhead. Use cross-over steps to get more quickly into position to return the deep lob.

CHALLENGE

How many of ten balls can you return to the center service T?

PRACTICE POSITION

THE PREPARATION

THE HIT

THE FINISH

Commom Faults

- The tossing partner does not stand off to the side when tossing.
- The partners are too far back away from the net.

- The player forgets to turn sideways.
- The hitting elbow is not at shoulder level in time.
- The toss is not high enough to give the hitter time to adjust the feet to the ball.
- The player neglects to adjust the body position to the ball. (Don't get set too soon. Good foot movement is a key to a good overhead. The key is to keep the ball in front of your body. Try catching a few tossed balls while in the ready-to-hit position to check your body alignment.)

- The player tries to hit the ball too hard and overswings.
- The player neglects to use a good wrist snap.
- The player pulls the head down and thus takes the eyes off the ball, which commonly occurs when the ball gets behind the player or drops too low.
- The left arm swings out to the left.

- The player uses too much follow-through and thus neglects the wrist snap.
- The player is off balance and thus brings the back foot around. (The player must learn to hit with the racket head and not with the body.)
- The player dips one of the shoulders instead of keeping them level and turning forward.
- The player bends forward from the waist.

CHAPTER 3 Playing the Game

Now that you understand the basic strokes of tennis and can keep a backcourt rally regularly in play for six to ten hits, you are ready to begin playing the game.

Tennis etiquette, basic rules, and scoring are presented as an introduction to basic tennis strategy.

THE ETIQUETTE OF TENNIS

Most of the following examples of conduct are reflected in **The Code** of ethical tennis behavior. Although the complete Code is not presented, the essentials of conduct and line call responsibilities are included in this section.

Player Conduct

Good sportsmanship is the key to tennis etiquette. Treat others as you desire to be treated. The following specific rules will make tennis more enjoyable for you and for those around you:

1. Know your opponent. Before you play, greet your opponent and introduce yourself.

2. Spin your racket to decide the choice of serve and side *before* you walk onto the playing court.

3. After a brief warm-up (10 minutes maximum), ask whether your opponent wishes to practice any serves. All practice serves should be taken by both players *before* any points are played. Never agree to simply play the "first serve in."

4. Begin the point as a server only if you have two balls in your hand or on your person.

5. Don't serve until your opponent is ready.

6. Observe the foot-fault rule. Failure to do so is considered a breach of tennis etiquette.

7. Keep score accurately and, when serving, announce the score periodically.

8. Return only balls that are good, especially on the serve.

9. Call the balls on your side of the net (promptly say "out" if the ball is out), and trust your opponent to do the same. Call faults and lets loudly and clearly. If the ball is in, or *if you are unsure, you must play the ball as good and say nothing.*

10. Talk only when pertinent to the match and only when the ball is not in play. However, acknowledge a good play by your partner or opponent.

11. Control your emotions and temper.

12. After each point, collect all balls on your side of the net and return them directly to the server. Don't lean on the net to retrieve a ball—the net cables may break.

13. Leave no balls or debris on the court when the match is completed.

14. Retrieve balls from an adjacent court by waiting until the point is over and then do so politely, saying "Thank you" or "Ball, please."

15. Return balls from an adjacent court by tossing or rolling them to the nearest player *after* the point in progress has been completed.

16. Call a let when there is reasonable interference during play (such as another ball entering your court).

17. Make no excuses. At the conclusion of play, shake hands with and thank your opponent for the match. Congratulate your opponent if he or she has won.

18. Don't monopolize the courts if others are waiting to play. Either play doubles or rotate at the conclusion of each set.

19. Always dress properly—be neat and wear a shirt.

Spectator Conduct

Whether you are a casual spectator watching an informal match or a member of a large crowd watching a championship tournament, you should be aware of some unwritten rules. Player concentration is essential to top performance, and anything that detracts from concentration could affect the outcome of an entire match. The general rule is the Golden Rule—govern your actions as you would have others act if you were playing. Follow these specific rules:

1. Remain seated in the areas provided for spectators. Never sit on any benches or seats within the fenced area unless you have a specific function.

2. Keep quiet during points. Nothing is more disturbing than unnecessary conversation.

3. Applaud good play only *after* the point is completed.

4. If you are interested in the score, keep score yourself. Do not continually bother the players by asking the score.

5. If you disagree with a decision, keep your opinion to yourself.

6. Referee a match only if acting in official capacity. (If you are asked to serve as umpire or linesman, you should do so willingly.)

7. If you are heading for another court, walk inconspicuously behind the fence of the court at the conclusion of the point.

Tournament Conduct

It is a privilege to have your entry accepted into a tournament. Here are some ways to show your gratitude.

1. Report to the tournament desk at least 15 minutes ahead of the scheduled time. If you cannot, let the tournament desk know ahead of time that you may be late or must default.

2. As the winner, return all balls to the tournament desk, report the score, and ascertain your next playing time.

3. Offer to help the tournament committee (with calling lines, preparing courts, transportation, etc.).

4. Thank the tournament director at the end of the tourney. If room and board were provided, adequately thank those responsible.

The Point Penalty System

Use of the U.S. Tennis Association (USTA) **Point Penalty System** is mandatory in any sanctioned tournament at district or sectional championship level or above. In other tournaments its use is at the discretion of the referee, who—before the start of the tournament or of any round or any match—may order its use. The purposes of the system are (1) to ensure continuous play, (2) to deter unsportsmanlike conduct, and (3) to ensure on-time appearance for matches.

1. The following rule violations relate to continuous play and result in point penalties:
   a. A player or team takes more than 25 seconds between points.
   b. A player or team takes more than 90 seconds to change sides.
   c. A player or team takes more than 3 minutes to resume play after an injury.
   d. A player prolongs an argument longer than 25 seconds after having been directed to resume play. (If a time violation has been penalized, the passage of an additional 25 seconds is the basis for an additional penalty.)

2. The following code violations relate to unsportsmanlike conduct and result in point penalties:
   a. Visible or audible profanity or obscenity.
   b. Abuse (throwing or slamming) of racket, balls, or equipment.
   c. Verbal or physical abuse of a player or official.
   d. Coaching.

3. If a player or team fails to appear on time for a match, that player or team may be penalized as follows:
   a. Less than 5 minutes late—loss of service/end option, plus one game.
   b. Five to 10 minutes late—loss of service/end option, plus two games.
   c. Ten to 15 minutes late—loss of service/end option, plus three games.
   d. More than 15 minutes late—default

The point penalties are assigned as follows:

First offense—a warning (unless deemed flagrant, which may result in immediate penalty, including a default)

Second offense—one point

Third offense—one game

Fourth offense—default

THE BASIC RULES OF TENNIS

Server and Receiver

The players (or teams) stand on opposite sides of the net. The player who first delivers the ball is called the *server;* the other player is the *receiver.*

Choice of Service or Side

The choice of side (that is, who plays on which side of the net) for the first game and the right to be server or receiver in the first game are decided by toss. Generally one player spins a racket and the other player calls one of the options presented by the markings on the racket ("upside-down" or "right-side-up," "M" or "W," "number" or "no number," and so on). The player winning the toss may choose or require the opponent to choose—for the first game—either the right to be server or receiver (in which case the other player chooses the side of the net) or the side of the net (in which case the other player chooses the right to be server or receiver).

The service is delivered alternately from the right and left courts, beginning from the right court, and is directed into the diagonally opposite service court. At the conclusion of each game, the server becomes the receiver and the receiver becomes the server. Players change sides after each odd-numbered game in a set— that is, after the first game, the third game, the fifth game, and so on.

Faults

A player has two attempts to get the serve in play. If either of these attempts is not good, it is deemed a **fault.** The following are examples of faults:

1. The server fails to hit the ball into the proper court.

2. The server misses the ball in attempting to strike it. (It may be tossed several times without penalty.)

3. The ball served touches a permanent fixture (other than the net) or the server's partner before it hits the ground.

4. A foot fault is committed.

A **foot fault** is called for the following reasons:

1. The server touches the baseline or the court area within the baseline before hitting the ball.

2. The server changes position by walking or running before hitting the ball. (A server may jump at the serve, and one or both feet may be over the baseline, provided the server touches the playing court or line only *after* hitting the ball.)

3. The server serves from outside the area between the sideline and the center mark.

Lets

A **let** is a ball in play that touches the net, strap, or band and is otherwise good. When a let occurs on a service, the serve is replayed. When a let occurs during any other play, play continues uninterrupted.

A let is called when play is interrupted by such things as a ball rolling onto the court or a ball breaking during a point, or if the serve is delivered before the receiver is ready and the receiver has made no attempt to return that serve.

When a Player Loses the Point

A player loses the point for the following reasons:

1. The player serves a **double fault.**

2. The player fails to return the ball before it bounces twice (the ball may be hit before it bounces, except on the return of serve, or after it bounces once only), or the player does not return the ball into the opponent's court.

3. The player returns the ball so that it hits the ground, a permanent fixture (fence, umpire's stand), or another object that lies outside the lines that bound the opponent's court.

4. The player volleys the ball and fails to make a good return even when standing outside the court.

5. The player *deliberately* touches the ball in play with the racket more than once when making a stroke (a "double hit") or *deliberately* "carries" the ball. (If *not* deliberate, a double hit and a carry are both legal and the ball is left in play.) In doubles, the serve may be returned by only one partner.

6. The player touches the net or the ground within the opponent's court with the racket or anything the player is wearing or carrying.

7. The player volleys the ball before it has passed the net.

8. The ball in play touches the player or anything the player wears or carries *except* the racket.

9. The player throws the racket at and hits the ball.

10. The player deliberately commits any act that hinders the opponent in making a stroke.

Identifying a Good Return

A good return is identified as follows:

1. The ball lands on the line.

2. The ball touches the net, provided it passes over and lands in the proper court.

3. The player reaches over the net to hit a ball that, of its own accord, has blown or rebounded back to the other side, provided the player does not touch the net with racket, body, or clothing.

4. The player's racket passes over the net after the ball has been returned, provided the net is not touched.

5. The player returns a ball that has hit another ball already lying in the court. (Any balls lying on the court, such as a missed first serve, should be moved before play continues. *REMEMBER:* If a ball comes onto the court during the point, a let should be called immediately and the point replayed.)

6. The ball is returned outside the net post, provided it lands in the proper court. If the ball is good, the players say nothing.

7. A player cannot call a ball out that lands on the other side of the net. You never make the call for your opponent.

Order of Service in Doubles

In doubles, the order of serving is decided at the beginning of each set. The pair to serve in the first game of each set decide which partner shall do so. The other partner serves the third game. The opposing pair decide which partner shall serve the second game of the set. The other partner then serves the fourth game. This order is followed throughout the set so that each player serves every fourth game.

If a player serves out of turn, the correct player must serve as soon as the mistake is discovered. All points earned are counted. If a complete game is played with the wrong player serving, the order of serve remains as altered.

Order of Receiving in Doubles

In doubles, the order of receiving is determined at the beginning of each set. The receiving pair decide who is to receive the first point, and that player continues to receive the serves directed to that particular service court throughout the set. (This also means that that player receives every other point in every other game.) The other partner does the same to the serves directed to the other service court.

If a player receives out of turn, he or she remains in that position until the completion of the game in which it is discovered. The partners then resume their original positions.

THE SCORING OF TENNIS

The Scoring of a Game

Zero Points: When a player (or team) has no points, the score for that player (or team) is called **Love.**

First Point: When a player (or team) wins his or her (or their) first point, the score for that player (or team) is called **15.**

Second Point: When a player (or team) wins his or her (or their) second point, the score for that player (or team) is called **30.**

Third Point: When a player (or team) wins his or her (or their) third point, the score for that player (or team) is called **40.** When *both* players or teams have won three points, the score is called **deuce.**

Fourth Point: When a player (or team) wins his or her (or their) fourth point, the score for that player (or team) is called **game** unless the score after the previous point was deuce.

After Deuce: When the score is deuce, one player (or team) must win two consecutive points to win the game. The first point after deuce is called **advantage (ad).** If the *server* wins the first point after deuce, the score is called **"ad in."** If the *receiver* wins the first point after deuce, the score is called **"ad out."**

To help keep track of the correct score, the server should state the score just before serving each point. The server's score is *always* given first. For example, if the server has won two points and the receiver one, the server announces the score as "30-15." To avoid confusion, remember that if the total number of points played is an *even* number, the ball is to be served from the *right,* or deuce, side of the court; if the total number of points played is an *odd* number, the ball is to be served from the *left,* or ad, side of the court.

HINT: **No-ad scoring:** A **sudden death** method of scoring can be substituted for the standard game scoring described. This no-ad method is popular in many events, particularly school matches, since it cuts down the total playing time. Points are scored 1, 2, 3, 4, and the first player or team to score four points wins the game. There is no ad. In singles or doubles, if the score reaches 3-3, the receiver chooses the service court from which to receive. In mixed doubles, if a woman serves the seventh point, the woman on the other team receives; if a man serves, the other man receives.

The Scoring of a Set

Conventionally, the player or team first winning six games wins the set, provided the player or team is ahead by at least two games. (If the score is 5-5, or 5-all, play continues until one side gets two games ahead—7-5, 8-6, etc.) An average set takes about 30 minutes to complete.

Tie-Break Scoring. Tie-break scoring is common and is used in most events once the score in any set reaches six games all. The following system is used in the "twelve point" tie-break scoring:

Singles. The player who first wins seven points wins the game and the set, provided the lead is by a margin of at least two points. If the score reaches six points all, the game is extended until a two-point lead is achieved. Numerical scoring (1, 2, 3, 4, 5, etc.) is used throughout the tie-break game.

The player whose turn it is to serve is the server for the first point from the deuce court. The opponent serves the second (ad court) and third (deuce court) points. The original server serves the fourth point (ad court) and the fifth point (deuce court). Each player continues to serve two points in rotation until the tiebreaker ends.

Players change ends after every six points and at the conclusion of the tie-break game, at which time the final set score is called "7-6."

The tie-break game counts as one game for the ball change, unless the balls are due to be changed at the beginning of the tiebreaker. Then, the change is delayed until the second game of the following set.

Doubles. The procedure for singles applies in doubles as well. The player whose turn it is to serve is the server for the first point. Thereafter, each player serves in rotation for two points, in the same order as previously in that set, until the winners of the game and set have been decided.

Rotation of service. The player (or pair in doubles) who served first in the tie-break game receives service in the first game of the following set.

The Scoring of a Match

A match is completed when one person or side wins two of three sets. In top men's tournaments, however, a match often consists of three of five sets. A 10-minute break is mandatory if requested by either player or side between the third and fourth sets. In junior events of ages sixteen and under, a 10-minute break is mandatory between the second and third sets. An exception is that this break is optional for male sixteen-and-under tournaments, and is taken only if either player requests it.

Server has won:	Receiver has won:	Score is:	Service court:
1 point	0 point	15-love	ad
2	0	30-love	deuce
3	0	40-love	ad
4	0	game	—
3	1	40-15	deuce
3	2	40-30	ad
1	1	15-all	deuce
2	2	30-all	deuce
3	3	deuce	deuce
4	3	ad in	ad
3	4	ad out	ad
5	3	game (server)	—

CHAPTER 4   Basic Singles Strategy

You are ready to start playing a game. Tennis poses special challenges, but first and foremost it should be played for *fun!* Don't get too caught up in the result of a match. Play to enjoy tennis, and the results will take care of themselves. The player with sound strokes has a distinct advantage in a tennis match. However, it is essential to realize that strokes are only a means to an end. Proper strokes enable you to make the best use of strategy, and once you have learned them, you must try to use them as intelligently and efficiently as possible. Our discussion of basic singles strategy will touch on the use of the serve, the serve return, the backcourt rally, and net play. The proper court positions for each of these situations will be addressed.

SERVING AND RECEIVING POSITIONS

THE SERVE

Concentrate on getting a high percentage of first serves (at least 60 percent) in the service court. Hit the serve only hard enough to control it. Don't waste your first serve by hitting a **cannonball** aimed at the service line, missing, and having to hit an exceptionally soft second serve. Serve from a position just behind the baseline and near the center T. This places you in a home base that bisects the area where the ball might be returned.

THE SERVE RETURN

The serve return swing at this point is a forehand or a backhand drive. The techniques used for the stroke are identical to those presented for the basic forehand and backhand strokes in Chapter 2. Initially, your only emphasis will be on getting the serve back. Don't try anything fancy on the serve return, because you want to get the ball in play.

When waiting for the serve, assume a set position slightly behind the baseline that bisects the angle to which the serve may be hit. A general home base will be about 1 foot behind the baseline, with the outside foot just about on the inside alley T. You will adjust this home base to a particular serve. If your opponent serves hard on the first serve and you are having trouble returning it, start back a little deeper. If your opponent serves much softer on the second serve, you will want to move your home base to inside the baseline. (A common mistake for beginners is to "charge" at the serve. Instead, turn and let the ball come to you.) If the ball is served wide, try to move on the diagonal to reduce the angle to which the ball is served.

MOVE DIAGONALLY TO CUT ANGLE OF WIDE SERVES

**SET POSITION BISECTS POSSIBLE
ANGLE OF RETURN**

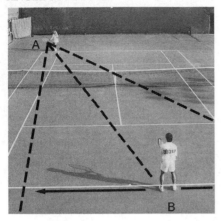

**BASIC TENNIS:
POINTS ENDING IN ERROR**

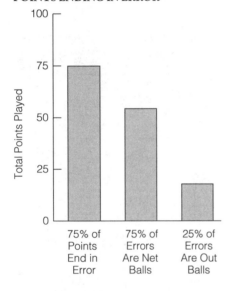

**CROSSCOURT:
NET IS LOWER, COURT IS LONGER**

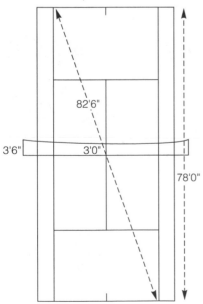

BACKCOURT TENNIS

Court Position

You must know where to wait for your opponent's shot in order to best return it. Assume a set position in a home base about 1 foot behind the baseline in a position that bisects the potential angle of your opponent's shot. For example, if the ball is being hit from the center of the baseline, your home base is essentially in the center of the court just behind the baseline. However, if the ball is being hit from Point A, assume a set position at Point B, slightly to the right of the center mark.

Stay Out of Midcourt. Do not get caught in **midcourt** unless you are purposely going to the net. Balls will bounce behind you or at your feet if you are in the midcourt. These are difficult shots to return, and you will usually be forced to hit them up (defensively). Less experienced players tend to overrun the ball. Because you are a novice player, let the ball come to you so you have more time to swing. If you have to run into midcourt for a short ball, return quickly to your home base 1 or 2 feet behind the baseline or go on to the net. Don't remain in midcourt.

Keep the Ball in Play

Make Your Opponent Hit the Ball. This is the first and foremost rule in tennis, for the advanced player as well as the beginner. Concentrate on keeping the ball going back to your opponent. Don't let your opponent off the hook by trying to hit the ball better than you have to, then missing or getting caught out of position.

Out-Rally Your Opponent. You need only hit the ball in the court one more time than your opponent to win the point. If you can keep the ball in play, your opponent may get in a hurry to end the point. This often results in a quick mistake and gives you an easy point.

Play Percentage Tennis

Try to balance your errors and placements. Unnecessary errors—balls that could have been returned—account for 75 percent of all points lost at the beginning level. On the other hand, only 25 percent are lost because of placements—shots hit so well they could not have been returned. The net is your biggest challenge. Three-quarters of the unnecessary errors are because the ball hits the net, and only one-quarter are because the ball lands out of bounds. The more difficult the shot you must return, the more you should think of the net as being "higher." Inevitably, you will make errors, but try to play **percentage tennis** and cut down on unnecessary errors. The player who wins is the one who makes fewer errors, especially at critical times.

REMEMBER: Never try to hit the ball better than you have to in order to win the point. In a nutshell, this strategy separates the players who win from those who lose. It is this difference that makes some players better competitors than others.

Use Crosscourt Shots. A ball hit diagonally across the court, as opposed to a ball hit parallel to the sideline, is a good percentage shot. The chance of error is less because the net is 6 inches lower at the center than at the sides and the court is 4½ feet longer from one diagonally opposite corner to the other. Also, your return of a **crosscourt shot** has less chance to "ricochet" wide off your racket if you return it crosscourt. The above reasons help explain why the crosscourt shot is your basic shot in a backcourt rally, and why this shot should be used to start almost all points from the back court.

Keep the Ball Deep

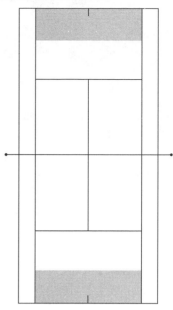

As you play more and encounter better players, you will find that simply keeping the ball in play is not enough. You must also keep the ball deep to prevent your opponent from reaching an offensive position at the net. A shot is considered deep if it lands within several feet of the baseline.

Your opponent can have difficulty responding aggressively to a deep shot because the hitting angle is reduced, which means you have less court to cover. Also, the ball takes longer to get to you, which gives you more time to prepare.

The ball should be returned high and deep (a **floater**) whenever you are in trouble or out of position. This will give you time to recover into proper set position.

For the beginner who has not learned to hit the ball safely and powerfully, a deep ball must clear the net by 5 to 8 feet if it is hit from near the baseline. A beginner who hits from a greater distance behind the baseline may have to hit a lob—a ball that clears the net by more than 10 feet—to keep the shot deep.

The deep, floater ball bounces higher and forces a beginning or intermediate opponent to move substantially back from the baseline to return the ball. (A more advanced player who hits with more power must clear the net by only 2 or 3 feet on most shots from the baseline.) In general, the farther behind the baseline any player is, the higher the ball must be hit over the net to keep it deep.

REMEMBER: Depth is more important than power!

NET PLAY

As a beginner, you may end up at the net by accident, such as when you have to run forward well into midcourt and can barely return a short ball. Or, you may have plenty of time to get to the short ball, but choose to play it aggressively and remain at the net, hoping for a weak return. In either case, the volley and basic overhead are two of the mechanically simpler shots in tennis, so you should have little fear of being out of your element at the net.

Court Position

The key to good net play is proper court position. Assume a home base that is about two-thirds of the way back in the service square, and a little off center toward the side of the court from which the ball is being returned. (In singles, it is impossible to cover the entire width of the court, so you should be certain to cover the near sideline first.)

If the ball is hit so you can return it with a volley, you want to move diagonally forward and return it from as close to the net as possible. Then return to your home base.

If the ball is lobbed up to you, move back and return it with an overhead. Don't try to hit too hard; instead, emphasize placement on your overhead. Then return to your home base. Expect your opponent to try to lob more when he or she is returning the ball from farther behind the baseline or when you are close to the net. (Your opponent is less likely to lob when returning a shot from on or inside the baseline. When hitting from midcourt, your opponent will probably try to hit the ball past you rather than over your head.)

PRACTICING BASIC SINGLES STRATEGY

Many elements of singles strategy, such as how to move to the ball, recovering to a home base after each shot, returning a deep ball high, and keeping your shot under control, are practiced as you hit the basic strokes. A very fine line exists between your execution of basic singles strategy and more advanced strategy drills, which are discussed in detail in Part 2 of this book. The following CHALLENGES help you to review some relevant concepts for basic singles strategy.

The Server's CHALLENGE

How many of ten balls can you serve into the proper service square? When you average seven of ten, put a target (cone) near each **T**. After you hit one cone, aim for the other.

The Receiver's CHALLENGE

While one player is serving, another player can be practicing returns. At first, try only to get the return back in the playing court with a corrected finish. As you improve, how close can you come to hitting a target (cone) that you place on the opposite side of the net?

The Backcourt Rally CHALLENGES

1. Begin playing rally points using the service squares. You will quickly see the importance of keeping the ball in play and of making your opponent move to return your shot. Also, some of the advantages and liabilities of crosscourt versus down-the-line shots become readily apparent. (*HINT:* You are not permitted to win the point by hitting hard or using an aggressive volley.)

2. Progress to rally points using the full court. You will learn the importance of returning to the proper home base after each shot and keeping the ball in play.

    a. Begin the rally with a crosscourt shot.

    b. As you improve, concentrate on keeping the ball high and deep over the net.

    c. Learn to anticipate that a short return often results from your hitting either a high and deep shot to your opponent or one that makes your opponent run. Be ready to come to the net if your opponent's return lands short. At the beginner's level, a shot to your opponent's backhand will probably be more effective than one to his or her forehand.

    d. Once at the net, be ready to end the point with a volley or overhead. If the balls are regularly returned over your head while at the net, realize that your home base is probably too close to the net.

The Playing CHALLENGE

Start the points with a serve. Incorporate scoring by playing games.

CHAPTER 5 — Basic Doubles Strategy

Doubles is a game of *position*. Each partner is primarily responsible for his or her side of the court and should be able to cover any return hit by opponents, as long as he or she knows where to be in a particular situation. The discussion begins by describing each player's basic starting position and how that player moves from home base by adjusting his or her position to the most commonly occurring situations.

STARTING POSITIONS

The Serving Team

STARTING POSITIONS

The *server* must stand behind the baseline, generally near the center of the server's side of the court. This allows the server to be in position after the serve to get to any ball returned to that side of the court.

The server's partner should start in a position at the net. The net player's home base position is approximately 10 feet from the net and about 2 feet from the alley.

The Receiving Team

The receiver should assume a home base that bisects the angle to which the server may hit. (Usually this is with 1 foot in the alley, but it may vary somewhat depending on whether the server is close to the center or wide, by the alley.) The receiver should begin the match standing near the baseline. If the opponent regularly serves very hard, the receiver must move back a couple of feet. If the opponent serves quite soft, such as on a second serve, the receiver can elect to stand a couple of feet inside the baseline. (If starting from inside the baseline, the receiver should either move back after the return or—if the serve is very short—use the return as an approach shot and move up to the net with his or her partner.)

The *receiver's partner* should begin by standing on the middle of the service line on his or her side of the court. This is only a temporary position. If the return inadvertently goes to the opposing net player, the receiver's partner should try to cover the center of the court. If the return is good (that is, back to the server), the receiver's partner should move up to the net player's usual home base while the point continues.

The primary responsibility of the net player is to prevent any balls from passing by on the alley side of the court and to force all balls to the middle. In addition, the net player should be constantly looking for the **poach**—that is, a ball that can be intercepted and cut off.

41

THE CROSSCOURT RALLY

The rally follows the serve and return, and the original starting positions change depending on what happens during the point. Practice CHALLENGES are presented to help isolate the four situations that represent about 95 percent of what can happen during a point in basic doubles. Understanding the following situations can make it easier for a player to learn to recognize what position to take on the court.

The Backcourt Players

Basic doubles play begins with the crosscourt rally, since the server must direct the serve diagonally across the court to the receiver. The primary objectives of the two *backcourt players* are to keep the ball away from the net players and to rally back and forth to each other. The backcourt players should try to keep the ball high enough over the net so that it lands deep in the opponent's court. The best way to do this is to hit a high, floating ball rather than a "beeline" ball that barely skims the top of the net. After each shot, the backcourt player returns to home base about 1 or 2 feet behind the baseline, at a point that bisects the potential angle of the opponent's return.

The Net Players

The *net players* "move with the ball" by sliding toward the side of the court to which the ball is returned. This ensures coverage of the appropriate alley as well as the opposing center of the court. In the photograph, player A has returned the ball to player C. Net player B moves toward the alley to prevent player C's return ball from going down the alley. Net player D moves toward the center of the court in order to cover the middle in case partner C should inadvertently return the ball to net player B. The net players should watch the ball at all times except when their partner is serving.

NET PLAYERS MOVE WITH THE BALL

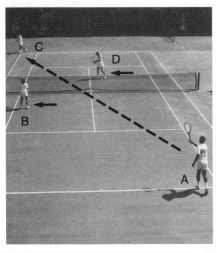

CHALLENGE

Situation #1: Net Players Move with the Ball

The backcourt players begin a crosscourt rally and try to keep the ball away from the net players, who are primarily concerned with "guarding their alley." While always watching the ball, the net players slide a couple of side skips toward the side of the court to which the ball is hit.

HINT: Rather than play the point to conclusion, stop the rally as soon as (1) both net players are moving routinely in the proper positions or (2) anyone gets out of position. (The point stops if something is incorrect, such as a player out of position. The position is corrected before resuming play.) After every two or three corrected points, each player rotates one position clockwise, thus allowing all players to practice in each position.

The Short Ball

If a return goes short, the backcourt player (C) moves into midcourt to return it and moves up to join his or her partner (D) at the net, instead of remaining in midcourt, where most balls bounce. The objective in doubles is to get to the net with your partner because (1) there is extra angle to which to hit, since you are up close; (2) you can get the ball back to your opponents much sooner, thus giving them less time to prepare; and (3) you can often hit down on the ball. Therefore, not only do the partners of the server and receiver start at the net, but the backcourt player joins his or her partner at the net *whenever he or she can get there and be set by the time the opponent hits the ball.* A short ball is the first of three examples in which a backcourt player should join his or her partner at the net. (If you must move well inside the playing court to return the ball, you have to take only a couple of more steps to go all the way to the net.)

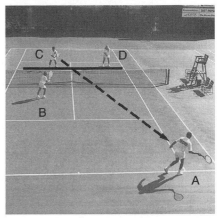

**THE SHORT BALL:
NET PLAYERS' NEW HOME BASES**

CHALLENGE

Situation #2: The Short Ball

Begin a crosscourt rally. When a ball lands short (near or inside the service line), come in and join your partner at the net in the new home base just inside the service line.

HINT: When both partners are together at the net, stop the rally and check and correct positions. Then begin another point.

When Both Partners Are at the Net. When both partners (C and D) are at the net, such as when the backcourt player moves up to return a short ball, each is responsible for every ball on his or her respective side of the court. Thus a new home base must be established a little farther from the net—about 15 feet instead of 10 feet. Although the net players have now sacrificed some volley angle, they can still move forward to hit the volley before it gets too low. Also, by putting their rackets in the air and moving a couple of steps back, both partners should be able to use their overhead to hit any lobbed ball before it bounces on their side of the court.

Any time the opposing net player(s) can move in and smash the ball down, the opponent(s) at the net should move quickly back toward the baseline to avoid getting hit and to have more time to react to the ball.

If a short return is successfully followed by another short ball, all four players may end up at the net. The objective then is to try to keep the ball low to prevent your opponents from smashing down and to enable you to move in and hit down.

THE LOB

The Short Lob

During the course of a crosscourt rally, one of the backcourt players may attempt to hit a lob over the opposing net player's head. The lob is not always successful and may go short, giving the net player a chance to hit an overhead. When a lob goes short, the following occurs:

1. The net player (D) immediately says "mine" so the partner (C) knows that the net player is taking it.

2. To avoid being hit and to gain time to react, the lobber's partner (B) moves back from the net as far as possible before the opponent hits the overhead.

3. Since the lobbed ball is high, it is in the air long enough to give the partner of the player hitting the overhead (C) time to get to the net and be set before the overhead is returned. (Both net players must remember to adjust to their new home bases farther back in the service squares.) The short lob is the second of three examples in which a backcourt player has time to join his or her partner at the net.

THE SHORT LOB

CHALLENGE

Situation #3: The Short Lob

Start the point with the basic crosscourt rally. After two or three returns, player A tries lobbing over the opposing net player. If the lob is short, the lobber's partner (B) retreats toward the baseline but gets set as player D smashes the ball, and the smasher's partner (C) joins player D at the net at the new home base.

HINT: After the overhead is hit, stop the rally and check and correct each player's position.

The Deep Lob

If the lob is hit as well as intended, it will go over the net player's (D) head. When this happens, the following occurs:

1. The lobbying player (A) can take advantage of what is usually thought of as a defensive shot by using the time the ball is in the air to join his or her partner (B) at the net. (Both net players must remember to adjust to their new home bases farther back in the service squares.)

2. The player who is lobbed over (D), on seeing that the shot cannot be reached, yells "switch" to his or her partner. The net player then crosses over to the other side of the court to be able to cover the area the partner is leaving. The net player also moves diagonally back to behind the baseline, expecting the opponents to hit an overhead.

3. The backcourt partner (C) crosses over to the other side of the court to return the ball. (The backcourt player must realize that the lobbed ball will bounce high, therefore necessitating a retreat well behind the baseline in order to let the ball drop down from the peak of its bounce to approximately waist level.) The ball is returned as a high lob, since the player realizes that both opponents are probably at the net and that his or her partner must have time to get back to the baseline.

Once both partners are side by side, either at the net or at the baseline, they stay side by side. If one goes back for an overhead, then the other also goes back. If one moves in for a short ball, the other moves in also.

The deep lob is the third example in which a backcourt player has time to come to the net.

THE DEEP LOB

CHALLENGE

Situation #4: The Deep Lob

Remember, the deep lob is used as a means to get to the net. If the lob is over the net player's head:

1. The net player (D) yells "switch" and crosses diagonally to the other side of the court toward the baseline.

2. The net player's partner (C) covers by crossing behind the baseline in an attempt to return the ball with a high, deep lob.

3. The original player hitting the lob (A) joins partner B in the new home base at the net.

HINT: When the lob goes over the net player's head, stop the rally, and check and correct each player's position.

**WITH AN INSTRUCTOR (A):
THREE ON, THREE OFF**

Practicing When an Instructor Is on the Court

The instructor becomes player A, and the remaining three players rotate around the instructor. If six students are on the court, divide into two three-player "teams." Team 1 plays the first two or three points, and Team 2 plays the next. The instructor always stays in, and each time a team returns to the court, its players rotate clockwise one position. After six rotations, all players will have played each position, and the instructor can then move on to practice the next situation. The advantage of having the instructor on the court is that he or she can better control the course of the point.

CHALLENGE

Play Random Rally Points

After all players have played each position in all four situations, the instructor can keep each team on the court for three or four points at a time and randomly introduce a different situation with each rally.

HINT: Play some random points with the instructor (player A) in the ad court. Begin playing points to their conclusion. However, if a player gets out of position, immediately stop the point and correct the position.

CHALLENGE

Add the Serve and Serve Return

Continue to play random points, but add the serve and serve return. The instructor begins by serving all points—two to the deuce court, then two to the ad court. After the four points have been played, the players rotate clockwise to the next position. After the three students have played each position, they each serve two points—one to the deuce court and one to the ad court. Finally, a regular twelve-point tiebreaker can be played.

At the conclusion of each point, each player should analyze where he or she is standing relative to the proper court position for the situation that presented itself. Remember that the receiver's partner moves from the service line to the proper home base at the net if the return has been hit back to the server.

HINT: A short serve should be played like any short ball—the receiver should follow the return to the net.

The three times a backcourt player may come in to join his or her partner at the net—in other words, any time he or she can get to the proper home base position and be set before the opponents can contact the ball for the return:
1. A short ball off the crosscourt rally
2. A short lob to the partner at the net
3. Following a deep lob over the opposing net player's head

PART 2

The More Advanced Tennis Player

CHAPTER 6 Advanced Stroke Considerations

There is no magic point in your tennis development at which you should begin learning stroke refinements and additions. The more you practice and the more you play, the quicker you master the basic forehand and backhand drives, the basic serve, and the basic net shots. You will probably develop personal style idiosyncrasies, which may differ from the text presentation already given.

Your strokes will develop more rhythm, and you may begin to use a more fluid (circular) backswing on your **groundstrokes.** As you gain confidence, you also begin to hit the ball harder. To avoid losing control of the harder-hit ball, you need to give it more spin—more overspin (**topspin**) and even **underspin** on the groundstrokes, and **sidespin** and topspin on the serve. On the forehand, for example, you may find yourself turning your basic forehand grip (Eastern grip) a little more to the right (clockwise) on the racket handle (**semi-Western grip**). This makes it a little easier to get additional topspin and may naturally lead to a circular backswing, with a slightly closed racket face. To get spin on the serve, turn your basic forehand grip a little more toward your left (counterclockwise), so it is slightly toward a backhand grip (**Continental** style).

Tactically, you should be able to put more emphasis on attacking. Realize that the basic strokes are only a means to an end. Much more important in determining success will be how the strokes you develop are used in a playing situation. However, to prepare for our discussion of more advanced singles strategy (Chapter 7) and doubles tactics (Chapter 9), let us look at variations of the basic strokes, beginning with backcourt play, followed by variations of the basic serve, and finally a more detailed description of the mechanics of net play.

Backcourt Play

THE FOREHAND

The Circular Backswing

In Chapter 2, a straight backswing was presented—simple to execute and certainly adequate for the beginner. As you gain more experience, however, you will become less mechanical in producing your stroke. You may naturally begin to use a more circular backswing.

It is easy to learn a circular backswing. Begin in the set position, with elbows bent so the racket head is at chest level (as for a volley). When you turn, first "think" the tip of the racket head back (in other words, don't let your wrist drag the racket back). Your arm should be relaxed at the elbow, although the elbow remains comfortably close to the body. Coordinate the backswing with the shoulder turn so they occur together.

When you have brought the racket almost all the way back, the racket head should be up near the shoulder, and the arm is not yet straight. You can still run comfortably with the racket in this position.

As you transfer your weight into the hit, your arm straightens a bit, to allow the racket to drop into hitting position below the ball. Dropping the racket head in an uninterrupted motion below the ball may take a little longer, but you will soon sense the basic rhythm and be able to adjust your timing. The racket drop gives the swing an inherent rhythm as well as speed. It also makes it easier to adjust to the lower ball. How far the racket drops depends simply on how low the ball is and how much topspin you wish to put onto the return.

As the swing continues, the racket head comes forward and up to the contact point, and finally toward the finish position.

THE BACKHAND

Hitting "Through the Flight of the Ball"

The "flight of the ball" is determined by where you aim above the top of the net in order to make the ball go to the desired court depth on the other side. The concept truly defines the path of the racket on the forward swing. You should position the racket at the end of the backswing (ready-to-hit position) so that the racket, as it begins to move forward, can swing as far as possible out and into the flight of the ball. (Another way to ensure that the swing is through the flight of the ball is to aim the racket heel in the ready-to-hit position to the level above the top of the net to which you wish to hit the ball. As an example, the racket head is much lower when you wish to lob than it is on a normal shot.)

As long as the wrist remains firm with the racket face beveled perpendicular to the flight of the ball, the ball will go into the desired trajectory. On the finish, relax the back leg so you can come up onto the tip of the toe; the sole of the rear foot faces the back fence. This ensures a smooth, fluid, and complete swing.

Using Spin on Groundstrokes

Perhaps you have noticed how much you can make the ball curve by throwing it with spin. In tennis the ball can easily be hit to give it spin. In fact, the basic forehand and backhand drives as previously presented will produce a certain amount of overspin (topspin). Such spin can be used to the hitter's advantage to gain more control. This is necessary, for as the ball is hit harder, the force of gravity is less effective in pulling the ball down to the court.

THE SEMI-WESTERN FOREHAND

THE GRIP

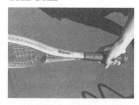

A HIGHER BACKSWING

A LOWER START

FINISH HIGHER

Topspin (or Overspin) Groundstrokes

Topspin can be put on the ball by swinging from low (waist level or below) to high (head level or above). The resultant spin allows the ball to clear the net higher and yet still drop quickly into the playing court.

The tip of the racket head must follow out into the flight of the ball after contact. This allows the racket to come around the outside of the ball, the side of the ball farthest from your body. Begin to use a deeper knee bend on your groundstrokes. As you contact the ball you can rise up into the shot somewhat. The "bend and lift" action is important as you add power and topspin. (Be careful that you do not pull your racket off the flight of the ball too quickly.)

The more topspin you use, the more the ball tends to drop short. Additional topspin is advisable when playing on a slow court, such as clay, where deep shots aren't so important (your opponent is less likely to attack the net on a short ball), and where longer backcourt rallies are common. More topspin is needed when you wish the ball to drop or dip quickly, such as when you want to pass the opponent at the net or hit the ball sharply over the net player's head (a topspin lob).

The Semi-Western Forehand

The semi-Western forehand is used by many players to gain additional topspin. The racket head begins its forward swing from a position considerably lower than the wrist and with the racket face more closed or flat. The finish is higher, meaning a steeper trajectory on the forward swing. The elbow bends more on the finish, which makes it appear that the wrist has actually "rolled over" the ball.

The Open Stance Forehand

Most top players, especially those who use semi-Western forehands, are now often hitting their forehands without stepping into their shot. Rather, these players hit their forehands with both feet remaining essentially parallel to the baseline and use a substantial shoulder turn and a strong thrust from their right leg to gain significant topspin and power. This shot also affords more efficient recovery, because an extra step is eliminated. The open stance forehand is absolutely the best forehand to use on clay courts, where players slide into their shots (many top players are sometimes using the open stance on their backhand as well, especially on two-handed drives).

Backcourt Play (*continued*)

THE BACKHAND SLICE

Underspin Groundstrokes

The forehand is almost always hit with overspin. But overspin is not the only spin used to help give control to groundstrokes. It is just as natural to hit the backhand with backspin, or "underspin." Top players commonly use underspin on backhands when rallying from the backcourt. Since the racket head starts to move forward from a position above the ball rather than first having to drop below the ball, the swing is much shorter. This makes it easier to take the ball on the rise, such as on an approach shot. Also, the ball does not have to be hit so far in front of the body, an advantage when you are hurried. The underspin ball can be hit with a great deal of pace and penetration, as on a slice, or it can be hit so softly that it tends to die on the court, as on a drop shot. It does not curve or dip downward as fast as with topspin, so the underspin is not nearly as effective as a passing shot against a net rusher.

How to Slice

For the slice, the racket starts high (at shoulder level), with the racket face beveled slightly open. The swing is forward and down. Ball contact is quite flat, with the racket face opening on contact. The swing continues out through the flight of the ball. The wrist stays firm and the follow-through is still high, with the wrist at eye level and the racket face still beveled open. Bending your knees to bring your body down to the level of the ball is important and prevents you from chopping down at the ball.

The Drop Shot

The drop shot is another variation of underspin. This shot softly clears the net and lands short in the court. It is used to pull the opponent to the net and can produce a winner if the opponent is too deep in the court.

For the drop shot, the racket starts well above the wrist and the backswing is very short. The forward hitting motion is down and under the ball. As the racket comes under the ball, open the racket face enough to give the ball a slight upward and forward lift; keep the wrist firm. The racket finishes at eye level, with the face still beveled open.

The trajectory of the swing is much steeper than with the slice, since pace and ball speed are actually negative factors on the drop shot.

THE FOREHAND DROP SHOT

THE DRIVE RETURN

The Serve Return

The use of the serve return and court positioning are discussed in Chapter 4. The following is a brief discussion of the mechanics of returning the serve and the resultant spins that can be used. The serve return motion is relatively short—somewhere between a high volley and a regular forehand or backhand. To help keep your backswing short, remember two things. First, make a full shoulder turn and step onto the foot nearest the ball; this gets the racket back. Second, on the backhand, keep the hitting elbow well away from your body (in front of it) during the shoulder turn. On the forehand, keep the elbow close to the body.

A straight backswing takes the racket back for most serve returns. The racket goes back at about chest level rather than at waist level, since the ball will generally bounce higher than on a normal drive. This allows you to position the racket so you can still hit through the flight of a higher-bouncing ball. As you turn, stay forward on your toes and lean a little forward with the front shoulder. This position encourages you to transfer your weight forward into the shot as you hit. (Adjust your feet so you can step directly into the ball—avoid stepping across.) The ball must be met well in front of, and away from, the body.

The Drive Return

Meet the ball with the racket face beveled flat, or perpendicular to the flight of the ball. Lift the ball up slightly as the racket moves forward. Finish with the racket face perpendicular to the flight of the ball.

To get more topspin, drop the racket head slightly below the ball on the backswing, and finish higher above the ball.

The Underspin Return

For the underspin return, slightly open the racket face on the backswing and hit forward through the flight of the ball, beveling the racket face open on the finish. Finish with the wrist at eye level, as you do with a regular slice.

If you take a little pace off the ball and use a shorter swing, the underspin slice return becomes a **chip.**

THE UNDERSPIN RETURN

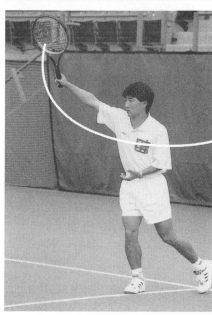

The Serve

THE GRIP

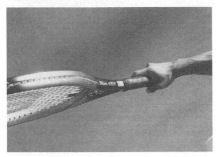

THE SET POSITION

Using Spin on the Serve

As you become more comfortable with the basic serve, you will gradually hit harder. If your more powerful serve prevents you from getting seven out of ten serves consistently in the court, you must learn to put some spin on the ball. All good players spin almost all their serves, because they gain considerable consistency for a small sacrifice in power. The spin allows the ball to clear the net higher, yet still drop quickly on the other side.

The Spin-Serve Grip

The first step in learning the spin serve is to change the basic forehand grip to one that is more toward the backhand, sometimes called the Continental grip. That grip allows you to brush up along the side of the ball more easily, rather than meeting it "flat on." Your initial serves using the Continental grip will probably land short and to the left. Don't get bogged down with swing and hitting details. Simply try to hit up on the ball more, and hit it farther to the right. This will give you a wrist hitting action that allows you to brush up and across the backside of the ball and results in a spin serve. Initially, you might try serving into a fence or backboard so that you aren't concerned only with results.

The Spin-Serve Ball Toss

The spin serve is divided into two parts: (1) the backswing (including the ball toss and the leg action) and (2) the forward swing.

During the ball toss and backswing, the body turns sideways more than on the basic flat serve. The full clockwise shoulder rotation allows you to "uncoil" during the forward swing. It also means that your tossing arm will make a letter **J** motion as it rises almost parallel to the baseline. The arc of the backswing may be shortened to help ensure a full shoulder turn. As you toss the ball, bend both knees forward; your heels will rise up from the court. The racket is now up and poised in a ready-to-hit position.

Different wrist hitting actions are used for the following three types of spin serves: the topspin serve, the American twist, and the slice serve.

THE BALL TOSS AND BACKSWING

THE FORWARD SWING

The Topspin Serve

The topspin serve is popular because the same basic hitting action is used for either a first serve or a second serve. Generally, a first serve is hit with more pace and less spin, since the server has a second chance to get the ball in the court. A second serve must still be hit with authority but needs more spin to give the ball a better chance of landing in the court. The discussion begins with the ball toss, which is made to a slightly different spot than in the basic flat serve or other kinds of spin serves.

Toss the ball a few inches in front of the baseline but slightly over your front shoulder (if the ball were to drop, it would land in front of your heel instead of in front of your toe). Allow the ball to fall a couple of inches from its peak. After the racket has dropped down behind your back, push up with your legs and swing the racket upward to meet the ball. (Think of brushing up and across the back of the ball with the racket.) As you contact the ball, reverse the wrist so the tip of the racket head goes forward, and finally out and over the top of the ball. **Pronation** of the wrist aids in obtaining pace when hitting a topspin serve.

You will now be a little off balance, so let the right leg fall across the baseline into the playing court on the finish. This, in turn, will result in the finish being to the body's left. The left arm should be tucked across the body. (The back shoulder comes forward later on the topspin serve than on the flat serve.)

HINT: To help learn the proper wrist action, practice the spin serve into the backhand side of the court. Also, don't let your wrist open up to allow the palm of the hand to face the sky on the backswing. If this happens and the wrist breaks prematurely, you will hit under and around the ball rather than up over the top of it.

The Serve (*continued*)

THE AMERICAN TWIST

The American Twist Serve

An extreme version of the topspin serve is the **American twist.** The ball is tossed farther behind the body, causing the body to bend farther back to reach it and creating an extreme "hitting up and over" reverse wrist action on the ball. The increased hitting up on the ball tends to make it kick up higher after it bounces. Since the ball is tossed farther behind you and therefore hit more on the inside of the ball, the wrist reverse makes it curve into the receiver as it approaches and then kick away in the opposite direction after it bounces. (The American twist serve can strain the back. Thus it is seldom used extensively. In addition, the excessive topspin tends to make the ball land short in the receiver's court.)

The Slice Serve

This sidespin serve is quite important, for it allows the right-handed player to serve wide into the receiver's right-hand service square (deuce court), and it allows the left-handed player to serve wide into the receiver's left-hand service square (ad court). The **slice serve** is distinctly different from the topspin serve in that the hit is around the outside of the ball rather than up the inside. Surprise is the key element. The easiest way to hit around the outside of the ball is to toss the ball to the right; however, that action makes it easier for your opponent to "read" what you are planning to do. Therefore, try to hit around the outside of the ball by tossing the ball more forward. A common fault is to pull down on this serve. Make sure your tossing arm, head, and body stay upright as long as possible during the hit. Also, when practicing the serve, don't be afraid to serve the ball too wide by using extra spin.

THE SLICE SERVE

THE FINISH

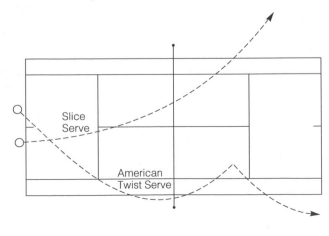

Slice Serve

American Twist Serve

Net Play

FOREHAND APPROACH VOLLEY

The Approach Volley

As you learn to hit harder and play more aggressively, you come to the net more often. In many cases, such as coming to the net after your serve, you must hit a transition volley from midcourt before getting to your home base position (10 to 15 feet from the net and slightly toward the court side to which the ball has been hit). *IMPORTANT:* Always be set when your opponent is contracting the ball so that you can change direction and react to the return. The simplest way to get set is to jump to a **split stop,** landing on the balls of both feet at the instant your opponent contacts the ball.

Read the return; then, while the ball is in the air, move diagonally forward to it with a couple of quick steps and balance as you step into the volley. The diagram below shows footwork for the forehand volley.

The approach volley will usually be low at your feet. On the low volley, lower the shoulder on the side of your body nearer the ball. This helps to get the racket head down to the ball without dropping the racket head. You may want to open the racket face slightly to put a little underspin on the ball and give it depth. Keep your wrist firm, meet the ball well in front of your body, and lift the racket forward into the flight of the ball with a short but smooth follow-through.

A half volley (a ball that bounces in midcourt just before contact) is played on the "short hop" and is hit like the low volley.

If the ball is high, you can move in more quickly after getting set. The racket may go back farther on the backswing, since you may turn more. *REMEMBER:* Since high volleys from midcourt are frequently hit into the net, hit out on the ball rather than down. The ball that is waist level or higher can be hit very flat.

BACKHAND APPROACH VOLLEY

FOREHAND APPROACH VOLLEY FOOTWORK

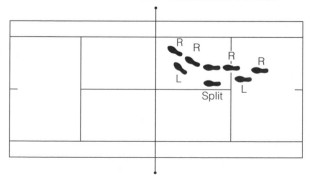

Net Play (*continued*)

THE DROP VOLLEY

The Drop Volley

Once you are at the net, you may find occasions when you want to drop the volley very softly over the net—for instance, when your opponent is deep in the playing court and his or her return is dipping low to you. For the **drop volley,** open the racket face on contact and relax your wrist. Use very little follow-through. This takes the speed off the ball and makes it land short. However, as in the drop shot from the backcourt, remember that your opponent will probably win the point if he or she can get to the ball.

The Deep Overhead

Any lobs landing near the service line should be hit flat or with little spin. Footwork is extremely important to hitting a good overhead. Turn by stepping back with your right foot, and use crossover steps to get into position. (In effect, you should be able to reach up with your left hand and catch the ball high and in front of your body.) Try to "set" on your back foot so you can transfer your weight onto the front foot as you hit.

When returning a deep lob, you may want to put some spin on the overhead to give it more control and play it almost like an approach shot. This will also help give you time to get back into position at the net for the next shot. If the ball goes behind you, the most effective way to transfer your weight and hitting shoulder into the shot is to use a scissor kick in midair, thrusting the right foot forward as you hit.

To recover most efficiently, let the left leg bend low and bend forward from the waist when landing from the scissor kick. This permits your right foot to step forward toward the net immediately after landing.

The Topspin Lob

The advance of first, the two-handed backhand and then the semi-Western forehand has helped to make the topspin lob a standard shot in every top player's repertoire. It is easy to disguise and adds a tremendous element of surprise to the lob.

To hit, let the racket head drop substantially below the ball on the backswing, and quickly brush or pull the wrist up and over the back of the ball on contact. Use a steep trajectory on your swing. *HINT*: At first, the balls will tend to land short, so think of "overhitting" the shot.

THE DEEP OVERHEAD

CHAPTER 7   Advanced Singles Strategy

The fundamental objectives of basic tennis strategy were presented in Chapter 4. The discussion of advanced singles strategy begins by emphasizing the importance of focused concentration. Detailed principles of the serve and serve return are then presented. The section on backcourt play reviews the fundamentals of court position, the importance of keeping the ball in play and keeping it deep, and then focuses on specific uses of crosscourt shots, down-the-line shots, and short balls. A thorough discussion of offensive tennis, including how to defend against the attack, completes the chapter.

ELEMENTS OF CONCENTRATION

Good concentration is the ability to channel or *focus* your thoughts on the immediate challenge. The mind tends to wander when faced with pressure situations, such as those created in athletic contests, schools, or jobs. When you are ahead in tennis, you tend to think about how close you are to winning the match or about who your opponent will be in the next round. If you are behind, you worry about the "stupid" shot you just attempted. Too often frustration shows; you begin looking back instead of ahead to the next shot or point. The player who concentrates well exhibits good body language—the head is up and the walk is brisk.

You can do several things between points to help prevent your mind from wandering. For example, take extra time, especially if you are losing the game or have just lost two points in a row. Rather than looking around—perhaps at players on the next court—keep your eyes on your court or on the strings of your racket. If you feel especially nervous, take a couple of very deep breaths (through the nose is more efficient than through the mouth) and exhale slowly.

Try to think in two-shot combinations. If you are going to serve and volley, bounce the ball a couple of times before you serve. *Visualize* where you are going to serve and where you will hit the volley (down the middle, to the open court, or behind your opponent). If you are receiving, get into your receiving stance, and don't look up at the server until you are completely ready to start the point.

If you are receiving against a backcourter, remind yourself to be patient: the longer the point lasts, the more determined you will be to not make a needless mistake. (The player who wins the majority of the long points usually wins the match.) Tell yourself to not try more than one risky shot per point. Remind yourself to be always ready for the short ball—to stand a step or two inside the baseline any time you have your opponent stretched out to reach a ball so that you can take the return early and get it back to your opponent quicker and perhaps get to the net.

Play Within Your Capabilities

The best player seldom attempts a shot he or she is incapable of consistently making. A player who concentrates well rarely tries a difficult shot if a simple shot will serve the same purpose. When a game nears the climax, make certain your opponent has to hit the ball to beat you—your ratio of errors versus forcing shots or winners becomes even more critical. On advantage points such as 40-30, don't gamble too much on your first serve, since the odds are probably with you, the server, anyway. However, if you are returning on any advantage point, you will probably play a little more aggressively and go for your best shot.

Play Ahead

Tremendous pressure is on your opponent if you are ahead. Since the deuce-court points are the ones that usually put you ahead or cause you to fall behind, concentrate on getting the jump on your opponent by not being careless in the deuce court. Play steadier in the deuce court. Get ahead with the first point and work hard on the third point—this can keep you from falling behind, or it can give you a commanding lead.

The first games in every set are important. Be ready to begin play. Don't make the mistake of "overhitting" early in the match until you find out whether or not your opponent can hurt you. (Overhitting is a common mistake made when playing an opponent that you think is a better player.)

If you haven't had many chances as the set progresses, when you finally get a chance, be aggressive and go for it! Don't let an opportunity pass by. The seventh game in each set is critical; the winner of the seventh game often wins the set.

CHALLENGE

Visualize a two-shot combination. For example, if you are playing against an opponent who serves and volleys, visualize where you will return the ball (forehand or backhand volley, or down the middle; whether you will stand in closer and chip the return, or stay far enough back to get a full swing at the ball). Visualize what you will do on the second shot—for example, hit a passing shot softly crosscourt or drive it hard down the line, or hit a high lob.

HINT: When you are returning a difficult shot, or if you feel a little tight or nervous, pretend the court is a little narrower. When "shrinking the court" in this manner, you still must hit your shot with authority and not play tentatively.

Practicing the Elements of Positive Concentration

Each point in a match is important. A close match may be lost by the player whose concentration "goes out" for only a couple of points. Good concentration is improved by (1) relaxing and taking your time, (2) focusing on the next point, even thinking of two-shot combinations, and (3) playing within your capabilities on each shot. The following suggestions have proven helpful in both learning and improving positive concentration.

1. Have a friend videotape one of your matches, keeping the camera on you, especially between points. When you review the tape, watch for poor and negative body language after points you lost (facial grimaces, etc.). Negative body language signals that you are thinking about what has already happened rather than about the next point.

2. Have a friend use a stopwatch to see how much time you take between points and when you change sides. Are you rushing when ahead or when behind? (Remember, you have 25 seconds between points and 90 seconds for change-overs.) If your opponent is obviously a better player, try to make the points, each game, and the match last as long as you can. Use the extra time to regroup your thoughts and focus on your plan of action for the next point or game.

3. Practice two-shot combinations to help you concentrate on playing with a purpose in mind:
   a. As the server, tell the receiver where you are going to serve and hit the first volley. (The receiver should return most serves to the middle of the court.)
   b. As the receiver, tell the server (1) where you are going to hit the return (for example, forehand or backhand volley) and (2) whether or not you are going to lob or try a passing shot.
      You might also decide to come in to the net on every second serve return.

4. Put a premium on being ready to play by shortening games and matches. This often makes it easier to focus concentration on the immediate objective. The following "scoring system" immediately handicaps the player whose thoughts drift from the task at hand.
   a. Starting games: Play a modified "set" in which (1) each "game" consists of three points, or (2) the first point in each game counts as two points.
   b. Starting matches: (1) Play four games or until a player gets two games ahead, or (2) play seven-point "matches."
   c. Finishing matches: Begin with the score at 5-5, and finish the set.
   d. Importance of each point: Play a "match" consisting of two out of three tiebreakers.
   e. Decreasing errors and "playing the score": Play points (backcourt or serve and volley) until one player makes two more errors than he or she has made placements. An error is "minus 1" and a placement is "plus 1." The score begins at 0-0. If player A makes an error on the first point, the score is "minus 1 to 0." If player B hits a winner on the second point, the score is "minus 1 to plus 1." If player A makes another error on the third point, he or she is then "minus 2" and the game is over.
      If the score is "minus 1 to minus 1," it is match point against both players, and an error will give the match away. If one player is ahead ("0 to plus 3," for example), that player can be a little more aggressive, since an error will only erase a plus and not cost the game.

CHALLENGE

"King of the Court" or "Bumper Tennis": In all of these drills, if you have an odd number of players and/or are using more than one court, you can:

1. Have the winner of each point or "game" stay in and the loser drop out. If you win three consecutive points or "games," you must rotate out. Keep track of all wins.

2. If you are with a group using several courts, after 15 minutes have the "high point players" on each court move up a court and the "low point players" move down a court. (This is not only a good "mixer," but also a great way to do a quick ability grouping.)

THE USE OF THE SERVE

The Importance of the First Serve

Your strategy as a server should be to get at least two-thirds of your first serves in the court. Don't waste your first serve just because you are entitled to another. Although it is true that you can serve more aggressively (and yet competitively) on the first serve because you have another chance, remember, if you miss that first serve, you are like a baseball pitcher falling behind the count on the batter. There is much less opportunity to take the offensive. The receiver knows this and will play accordingly, especially since your opponent then expects the second serve to go to the backhand.

On critical points, however, when it is important to keep the pressure on your opponent, a much higher percentage of first serves *must* be good, even if it means serving less aggressively.

If your second serve is not very effective (you win less than 45 to 50 percent of the points), you should try to get approximately 66 percent of your first serves in play. If your second serve is very effective (you win more than 50 percent of the points), you can be more aggressive and take more chances on your first serve.

Unless you are trying to serve to an extreme angle, depth is important, especially on a second serve. If the serve lands short, the receiver has many more options and can play much more aggressively, as described in the section on serve return.

Don't double fault. This is analogous to a baseball pitcher walking a batter.

Mix Up Your Serves

A hard, flat serve to the backhand may be your most effective serve, but you cannot use it all the time, any more than a pitcher would use only a fastball. Keep your opponent guessing and off balance.

Serve wide to your opponent in these circumstances: (1) You have a natural angle, such as a slice to the forehand in the forehand court or a twist to the backhand in the backhand court. (2) Your opponent undercuts (slices) most returns. This may mean your opponent cannot return well with the drive, the natural return for a wide ball, especially when hitting crosscourt. (3) Your opponent assumes a faulty set position—too far behind the baseline or too close to the center of the court. (4) Your opponent generally backs up or runs wide to return a wide serve instead of stepping in and cutting off the angle. (5) There is a letdown in concentration (after a long point or a long game).

Serve in tight to your opponent's body (for example, to the forehand in the ad court) if this occurs: (1) Your opponent normally takes a big swing at the return. A ball close to the body makes a big swing difficult. (2) You are in trouble, such as 30-40 and serving a second serve. A body serve not only cramps the return swing but also cuts down the chance for an outright winner with an angled return. Don't give your opponent the angle on an important point. (3) Your opponent often moves to the net behind the return of your second serve. Try to "handcuff" your opponent with balls served into his or her body.

Serve down the middle to your opponent (toward the center T) to reduce the angle on your opponent's return.

Serve high "kickers" (topspins or twists) to your opponent if (1) your opponent cannot return a high ball well (many players cannot hit well through a high ball); or (2) your opponent moves backward to hit the return.

Vary the Speed

Realize that some receivers rely on the speed of the hard serve for the effectiveness of their return. Don't hesitate to use more spin occasionally to slow the ball down, even on a first serve. If you want to serve hard, remember that the net is lowest in the center and the ball gets to the receiver sooner down the middle than when it is served wide. Also, your opponent has less angle for the return.

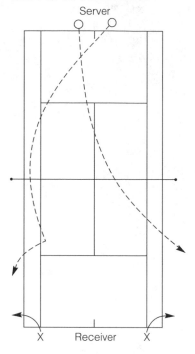

THE USE OF WIDE SERVES

Server

X   Receiver   X

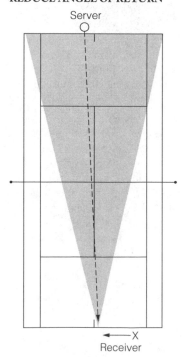

SERVE TOWARD CENTER T TO REDUCE ANGLE OF RETURN

Server

X
Receiver

THE USE OF THE SERVE RETURN

A good serve gives the initial advantage to the server, whether or not the server comes to the net after the serve. However, a good return can at least neutralize the advantage. In practicing receiving, work first to develop a consistent serve return and then to develop a return that can turn the point into an advantage for you.

Vary the Return

Although the basic return is usually a rather flat drive, vary your returns. Stand back a little farther sometimes, take a bigger swing, and drive the return with more topspin. (Against a net rusher, this can upset the serve-and-volley rhythm, since the server must take a couple of extra steps to get in to the ball.) Or, move in closer in order to hit the ball sooner (especially when your opponent has had difficulty serving and has been serving short), even to the point of occasionally going to net behind the return. Remember, the earlier you take the ball, the shorter the swing. You may also use more underspin, by using a slice or a chip.

Be Aggressive

Most of all, be positive. Look at returning serve as a challenge. Don't look up to return until you are really concentrating and mentally ready. (Sometimes, a deep breath at this stage helps.) Be on your toes; take a step forward, followed by a little jump up into the air just before the serve is hit, to help you get ready. There is no "batter's box" in tennis. Make the server know you are there. Move around. Make your opponent think of serving down the middle by standing wider in the court. Stand in close to make the server try to hit too good a second serve. Force the server to change the serving rhythm or spin by standing far back.

Make the server pay the price when a first serve is missed. It is reasonable to assume that the second serve will be to your backhand, and because the server is hitting it with more spin, it may be short as well. Be ready to move in and "chip and charge" to the net on the return, or—especially in the deuce court—when the server and volleyer tosses the ball up, move to your left and "crank" a forehand return down the line.

Have a Plan

Return to a spot. *Before* the ball is served, decide where you will return it and what kind of return to hit. Don't wait to see what kind of a serve it is and then react to it. Know ahead of time whether you will hit softly crosscourt to your opponent's backhand volley or whether you will hit hard down the line to your opponent's forehand.

Keep the pressure on the server in general by getting a high percentage of returns into play. But don't be afraid to "go for it" by hitting harder or closer to the line. (You can gamble more when you are returning serve, since the server usually has the advantage anyway. Remember, you only need to put together a couple of good shots to have a real chance to break serve.) When you get to "break point," be aggressive and go for it, since you may not get other chances.

If you are playing against an opponent who serves and volleys, if you can return the ball low and down the line, realize that the volley will probably be returned crosscourt (over the low part of the net and to the open court). If you return crosscourt, the volley may be hit to either your forehand or your backhand. Therefore, if you are returning from the ad court, return down-the-line if you want to have the best chance to hit a forehand passing shot or lob. If you'd rather return the volley with a backhand when returning from the ad court, hit your serve return crosscourt to increase the chance of the volley being returned to your forehand.

STAND IN CLOSE ON SOME SECOND SERVES

MOVE TO YOUR LEFT AND "CRANK" A FOREHAND RETURN

HINT: When playing an opponent who has a big serve but who does not serve and volley, it is imperative to keep the return of serve out of the middle of the court. This prevents the server from dictating the point with the second shot, usually a big forehand.

THE ZONES OF TENNIS

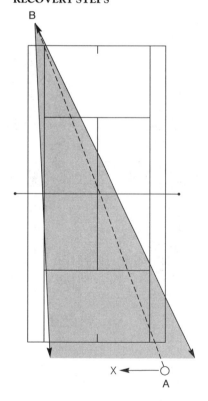

CROSSCOURT RETURN SAVES RECOVERY STEPS

BACKCOURT TENNIS

Basic singles strategy in Chapter 4 emphasized the importance of keeping the ball in play (playing percentage tennis) and keeping the ball deep. However, additional considerations are important for the experienced backcourt player. Imagine that the tennis court is divided into three zones: (1) the *defensive zone* (when hitting from more than 4 feet behind the baseline), (2) the *neutral zone* (when hitting from within 4 feet of the baseline), and (3) the *offensive zone* (when hitting from more than a couple of steps inside the baseline).

If you hit from within the offensive zone, you have the opportunity to attack and move to the net. If you are returning from the defensive zone, you are very vulnerable to the attack and are frequently just trying to stay in the point. However, when playing from the neutral zone, you constantly jockey with your opponent for position in order to hit a shot that will give you the chance to gain the advantage. The following are important considerations for playing in the neutral zone, or in other words, for playing smart backcourt tennis.

Change the Pace of the Ball

The outcome of a backcourt rally is often affected by the player who effectively changes the pace (speed) of the ball—either by changing spins or by using more or less power. Never hit more than three consecutive balls the same way, that is, using the same pace, spin, and trajectory. The mix of powerful shots with some off-speed topspin floaters or solid underspins makes it difficult for your opponent to maintain a hitting rhythm. Therefore, your opponent's ability to control the return, especially the depth, is reduced. Both the underspin and the high floater are good choices to use after two or three hard drives in order to elicit a short return and set up your net attack.

When to Hit Crosscourt

Use a crosscourt shot:

1. *To get your opponent moving:* Start the point immediately with a crosscourt shot. Your opponent must run more because a crosscourt shot can be hit to greater angles. The more your opponent has to run for a ball, the less chance he or she has to get set and therefore to transfer weight into the shot. The chance of a weak return is increased. Especially if you are hitting to a strength, a crosscourt shot will help to expose a weakness to the other side on the next shot.

2. *If your opponent hits down the line to you:* He or she will have to move a considerable distance to get to your crosscourt return. If you can return the down-the-line shot with an aggressive crosscourt, you have an excellent chance to win the point outright.

3. *When you are out of position:* The accompanying diagrams illustrate that if you (player A) return the ball crosscourt when out of position, you will have three or four fewer recovery steps to take to get back to your home base (point X), bisecting the possible angle of your opponent's (player B's) return.

When to Hit Down the Line

Use a down-the-line shot:

1. As a change of routine to the basic crosscourt pattern.

2. To hit to a player's weakness.

3. To hit behind a person who is running fast to cover the opposite side of the court.

4. As the basic attack shot to get to the net. (Usually you hit this ball early, since you want to get to the net as quickly as possible to give your opponent less preparation time.)

Because the ball travels a shorter distance and over a higher part of the net than with a crosscourt shot, and because it is more difficult to follow through the flight of the ball (the ball tends to slide off the racket to the side), allow more margin for error on the down-the-line shot. Use considerable spin and aim well inside the line when returning down the line from the neutral or defensive zone.

When to Hit Short

Basically you want to keep your opponent as far in the backcourt as possible. But many players don't move forward as well as they move to the side. Also, some players stay in the backcourt because they feel insecure at net. If your opponent never moves up to the net, try returning the ball short to force your opponent to come to the net. Once your opponent gets to the net, try lobbing—your opponent may be avoiding the net because of an overhead weakness.

You may also want to return short if your opponent is pulling you to the net and then successfully lobbing over you or passing you. If you are not effective when inadvertently pulled to the net, bring your opponent to the net first by using a soft, short ball instead of an approach shot. Also, short shots following high floaters can be effective change-of-pace shots.

The extreme short ball, called a **drop shot,** is hit with considerable underspin. The drop shot is commonly used when a player thinks it will produce an outright winner. You should seldom attempt it, except when hitting from midcourt (offensive zone), for if your opponent can get to it, a put-away will be the likely result.

DOWN-THE-LINE RETURN INCREASES RECOVERY STEPS

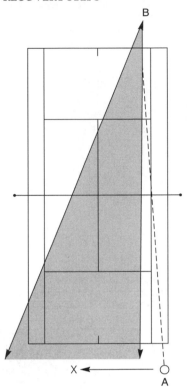

OFFENSIVE TENNIS

Approaching the Net on a Groundstroke

The section on backcourt tennis has shown how basically defensive maneuvers (deep balls or balls that move your opponent) can force weak or inaccurate returns, giving you the opportunity to move from the neutral zone to the offensive zone.

During a backcourt rally you might hit aggressively and record your share of outright winners. However, advanced players generally use a backcourt rally primarily to set up a chance to attack at the net. (Beyond the beginning levels, there is a much higher percentage of winning shots or forced errors hit by the attacker at the net than when both players stay in the backcourt.)

When to Approach the Net. When a short ball (weak shot) is hit to you and you must move into the midcourt offensive zone to return it, you can:

1. Play it 100 percent defensively by returning it fairly softly, high, deep, and down the middle—giving your opponent no angle for return and giving yourself time to retreat to a more comfortable position behind the baseline.

2. Play it as a drop shot, which tends to pull your opponent up out of position.

3. Play it 100 percent offensively by approaching the net. Even intermediate players can have reasonable success playing at the net (we have seen how mechanically simple the volley really is), provided they come to net at the right time with the right shot. This correctly implies that the most critical factor in successful net play is the method used to get there—the approach shot itself.

Anticipation is a learned response. The more you play, the more you learn to "feel" the kind of return your opponent may hit. Anticipation of the short ball helps make your approach shot easier. You must learn to "feel" when the return may be short (the result of a deep or hard shot, or because your opponent had to run a great distance and is stretched out wide). Be mentally prepared to move in quickly and assume a set position a step inside the baseline.

WHEN YOUR OPPONENT IS STRETCHING WIDE, ASSUME A SET POSITION ONE STEP INSIDE THE BASELINE

In today's trend toward power tennis, there is a greater emphasis on taking the ball early near the offensive zone with big, heavy topspin groundstrokes, especially on the forehand side. (Be alert for the chance to run around the short ball returned to the center of the court in order to hit a forehand "off court" to your opponent's backhand side.) Be quick to recognize the opportunity to move up from the neutral zone into the offensive zone. For the additional and more explosive power, a greater uncoiling of the shoulders and legs must be accentuated. The forehand approach shot can effectively be hit while running forward. Contact is made with the weight on the right foot, and then the left foot follows forward while finishing the stroke.

Think of getting to the net more often if:

1. The court is fast. This means your opponent will have less time to prepare to return your approach shot.

2. The wind is at your back. This gives your shot added speed and also hurries your opponent.

3. You feel your presence at the net may pressure your opponent into an error.

Where to Hit the Approach Shot. *Depth* is critical to an effective approach shot, for it substantially limits the angle available on the return. Limiting the angle is important, since a player cannot cover the entire width of the court when at the net. The deeper the approach shot, the more difficult it is to successfully return the ball crosscourt. There is less available angle to which to hit the passing shot, and it is mechanically more difficult to get the racket around the ball quickly enough to return crosscourt.

Thus, if the approach shot is hit deep, the net player can assume a set position closer to the sideline to which the ball is hit. By taking a step diagonally forward toward the near sideline, the net player should be able to cover any ball returned down the line. By taking a step diagonally toward the center of the court, the net player can cover most balls returned crosscourt. The deeper the approach shot, the more the net rusher should expect a lob and thus not get so close to the net.

Down the line is usually the best place to hit the approach shot. The net player assumes a position, about 15 feet from the net, that bisects the potential angle of return. If the approach shot is hit deep and down the line, the net player need stay only on that respective side of the court when going to the net. If, however, the approach shot is crosscourt, the net player has to move all the way across the center of the court to bisect the potential angle of return. There usually is not enough time to take the extra steps required to move across the court and still be set before the opponent returns.

A *crosscourt* approach shot might be used if your opponent has a definite weakness on that side, or if the net rusher feels a winner may be hit on the crosscourt approach.

A *down-the-middle* approach shot might be used (1) if the opponent has very good angle returns (since it diminishes the angles), (2) if the opponent moves very fast (it cuts down any natural speed advantage, since the opponent has no place to run), and (3) to increase the chance of a lob return (since there is little angle to which to hit the passing shot).

How to Approach the Net. When the return is weak or the chances for a weak return exist, your thoughts should immediately change from steadier play to "attack." At the same time, don't become careless when you finally have the opportunity to attack. Remember, you have worked the entire rally to get the opportunity to come to the net. Don't overhit. Don't rush. Be content to use the approach shot as an interim shot to set up the winning volley (unless you have an obvious opening).

Try to hit the ball early on the approach. Contacting the ball no later than at the top of its bounce gets you closer to the net, and gives your opponent less time to prepare for the return. It is an axiom that "the earlier a ball is met and the closer to the net you are, the shorter your swing need be." Most balls taken "on the rise" on the backhand side are hit with underspin by one-handers, because the underspin shot requires less backswing and is easier to "time" with the shorter swing. Also, the underspin ball tends to bounce low and often skids, forcing your opponent to hit up. However, more players will "pummel" the short ball if returning with a forehand or two-handed backhand.

Court Position. Follow the ball to the net. In other words, if you (player A) hit the approach shot down the line, go to net a little off center (toward the near sideline). This will help you bisect the potential angle of return of player B and best enables you to cover the shot.

Time your split so that both feet are on the court as your opponent contacts the ball. You then will be able to react efficiently when you see where the return is hit.

Come to net only when you feel you can get in close enough, commensurate with being completely set (usually about 15 feet from the net). This cuts down the potential angles of return (which are greater when you are farther from the net) but still allows you to protect against a lob.

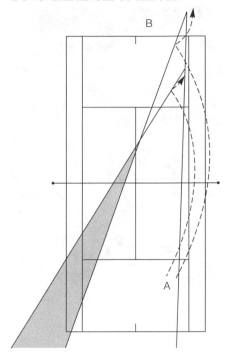

A DEEP APPROACH SHOT CUTS DOWN THE ANGLE OF RETURN

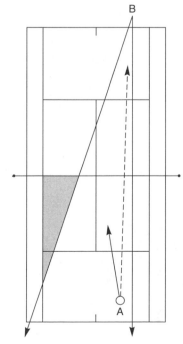

FOLLOW THE BALL TO THE NET

VOLLEYER "WRONG FOOTS" OPPONENT

Reacting to the Return at the Net. Footwork is important. After jumping to a split stop on the balls of your feet at the instant your opponent contacts the ball, take several quick, small steps forward and set again to hit your volley. Avoid large or lunging steps. If the ball is one large step away, take three small, quick steps to reach it so you can be balanced when you hit the volley.

In general, you should volley to the open side of the court. (If the opponent's return is hit down the line, volley crosscourt; if the return is crosscourt, volley down the line.) The premise is that your opponent will have to hit the passing shot on the run, which may decrease the chance of an effective return. The net player must be certain to move across the center of the court after the volley in order to protect the court from a return down the line.

However, as with an approach shot, if your opponent moves very fast and is also effective with angle returns, then you might want to play more volleys down the middle of the court or hit some behind the player. For example, if the opponent returns down the line, volley down the line; if the return is crosscourt, volley crosscourt.

Hitting behind the player ("wrong footing" your opponent) is very effective on a clay court or a slow hard court. (A ball hit to the open court gives your opponent a great deal of time to prepare on these surfaces.)

If the ball is low, the volley must be deep or very sharply angled. Take the low ball as early as possible so it doesn't have time to drop far below the level of the net. A crosscourt volley is a safer shot because it passes over the lowest part of the net and because the court is longer.

If the ball is lobbed very high, or if sun and wind are a deterrent, let the ball bounce before hitting your overhead. Otherwise, always hit it before it bounces. Hit the overhead aggressively from the forecourt (it is the most offensive shot in tennis), but play it with more spin when hitting from deeper in the backcourt.

Approaching the Net After Your Serve

Before you serve, make up your mind to either come to the net or stay back. Don't wait to see whether the serve is in or effective. Consider coming to the net in these instances: (1) You have a strong or effective serve. A forcing serve is more likely to elicit a weak and playable return. (2) You have a strong volley and overhead. An advanced player regularly may come to net behind both the first and the second serves. An intermediate player will occasionally come to net behind the first serve and rarely behind the second. (A beginner rarely will come to net behind either serve.) (3) You are playing on a relatively fast surface, such as a fast hard court or grass court. A fast surface can make your serve more effective, whereas a rougher surface such as clay can slow down the bounce of the serve so much that the receiver has ample time to prepare for a good return. (4) You are serving with a strong wind at your back. This also gives the serve more pace and thus gives the receiver less time to prepare. (5) Your opponent is becoming "grooved" into hitting one kind of return. If the receiver is not expecting you to come to net, the return ball will probably be kept deep by being hit fairly high above the net. This could give you a relatively easy volley. On the other hand, if you regularly have been coming to net behind your serve, the receiver will be trying to return the ball low, which would make it land short. If you occasionally stay back on your serve, you may have the opportunity to hit a forehand or backhand approach shot after this short return.

Coming to the Net Behind Your Serve. As the first step in getting to the net on the follow-through of the serve, bring your back foot across the baseline and into the court. Continue to move forward in the direction of the serve until your opponent contacts the ball. At that instant, you should be completely balanced and set by virtue of your split stop.

You should have time for three or four steps before coming to your split. This puts you in the vicinity of the service line, although behind it. You must accept the fact that, on your serve, it is impossible to get all the way to home base at the net from behind the baseline before the ball is returned. Therefore, you will have to hit one volley or half volley from the difficult and relatively vulnerable midcourt.

Remember to follow the ball to the net and make the initial split on the side of the court to which the ball has been served, so that you can cover the down-the-line return.

After you split, move diagonally forward with several small, quick steps to where you want to contact the ball. Set again for the volley. This should allow you to actually contact the ball in front of the service line.

Hitting the Volley. If there is an opening, you probably will want to volley to it to force the receiver to hit the passing shot on the run. For example, a wide serve to the backhand in the backhand (ad) court leaves the forehand court open—especially if the ball is returned down the line. If there is no obvious opening, play the shot conservatively and deep. (In fact, many good players volley essentially down the middle of the court in order to cut down the angle for the passing shot.)

If the return is down the middle and low, you are not yet close enough to put any angle on your volley, so the premium is on volleying deep. If the return is hit wide, you may be able to use more angle on your volley and therefore may not want so much depth.

After you have hit the first volley, follow the ball the rest of the way to the net, as you would when approaching on a groundstroke. (Remember, your home base is about 15 feet from the net toward the side of the court the ball is on.) If the return is low, treat the first volley like an approach shot—don't overhit the ball. The first volley should set up your second volley. If the return is high, move in close and "pound" the volley.

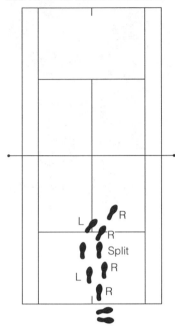

KEEP THE SERVE RETURN LOW

Defending Against the Net Rusher

How to Return Serve Against the Net Rusher. The primary objective of the receiver is to return the serve low and at the net rusher's feet. This forces the net rusher to volley up. This is usually a less offensive volley, since the shot can't be hit as hard. You will have to decide what kind of return is most effective. Here are a few suggestions:

1. Against players who have a volley weakness on one side or the other, you may want to concentrate on returning to the forehand volley or to the backhand volley, as the case might be.

2. Against players who volley very well when pulled wide—especially those with a great deal of touch or who may be very quick—you may want to return more balls down the middle.

3. The basic return should be a solid, fairly flat, or topspin drive; although against net rushers who prefer to volley a hard return, you may want to try some softer underspin or chip returns.

4. Try moving in when your opponent is getting too close to the net for the first volley. You can keep the net rusher from getting in so close if you take the ball sooner yourself. Perhaps you can beat such a player to the net by using the return of service as an approach shot.

5. Stand farther back than usual if you want more time to react. This also may upset the server's timing in coming in, since two or three more steps are needed before the volley. Keep the ball down the middle to minimize the chance for an angle volley, and be prepared to lob on the second shot.

6. Be aggressive when you get a chance to "break serve."

Above all, if you are unsuccessful in returning one way, change and try something different. Examples include standing in closer to or standing farther from the net, hitting harder or hitting softer, and hitting for more angle or hitting down the middle.

Once Your Opponent Is at the Net. Most important in defending against the attack: Do not be pressed into trying too good a shot against the net rusher. Don't feel you have only one shot in which to win the point. The axiom is "Make your opponent hit the ball to beat you." Your opponent does not win the point automatically simply by being at the net. It is remarkable how many "sure winners" are missed at the net. Unless you are confident of hitting an outright winner, use your first shot to pull your opponent out of position and open up the court; then, be more aggressive on the second shot. Take your time. Don't be rushed into not getting set or not staying down with the shot.

The Use of the Lob. Most players think only of trying to blast the ball past their opponent. Consequently, the lob is probably the most underused shot in tennis, yet it is one of the most effective. Give yourself plenty of margin (never miss a lob wide), and get the ball up high into the air. Any time you succeed in getting a lob over the net player's head, move into the net. Even if the lob doesn't get over the net player's head, if it is deep, it tends to push that player back away from the net and to open up the court in front of him or her for a passing shot.

Use the lob:

1. Whenever you are hitting from substantially behind the baseline in the defensive zone.

2. If the sun is a factor, even if you are not in the neutral or defensive zones.

3. On windy days. Although it is difficult to lob in the wind, it is even more difficult to hit an overhead in the wind. (Don't lob as high on windy days, and remember that it is easier to lob defensively when the wind is at your back.)

4. On hot days, particularly early in the match. If the match turns out to be a long one, conditioning could be a deciding factor: continually returning lobs is tiring.

5. Often on balls that are volleyed down the middle, even when returning from the neutral zone. (You don't have much angle for a passing shot.)

6. Occasionally on short balls. A surprise quick lob can be effective.

7. When your opponent closes too close to the net.

Adding topspin to a lob can be very effective, particularly if it is not an obvious lobbing situation or when lobbing against the wind.

The Use of Passing Shots. The most important principle in the use of passing shots is to keep the ball low so the net rusher will be forced to hit it up, decreasing the opportunity to make an aggressive volley. Topspin balls drop faster than flat or underspin balls. Therefore, most passing shots are hit with substantial topspin.

Most passing shots are hit *down the line*. The ball reaches the opponent quickly down the line and affords little time to prepare. Also, a player who is running to the side will have difficulty getting the racket around the ball fast enough to pass crosscourt. Since the net player is probably covering the down-the-line shot, you must hit the ball fairly hard. Try to stay forward with the ball as long as you can, and don't pull up from the ball with your body. After the shot, recover quickly, since the net player probably will try to volley to the crosscourt opening.

The *crosscourt* passing shot is a good one if you have the opportunity to hit it (for instance, when the ball is volleyed short). In general, use a lot of topspin to "roll" the ball over the net when attempting a crosscourt passing shot. If you keep your ball crosscourt, your opponent has less opening in which to volley and your shot has more time to drop low. It is less essential to hit the ball hard when you attempt to pass crosscourt than when you pass down the line. If your shot is soft and low, there is little the volleyer can do. Try the soft change-of-pace shot occasionally to pull your opponent in to the net and out of position enough to set up the passing shot or quick lob on your next hit.

LOB WHEN RETURNING FROM THE DEFENSIVE ZONE

USE A SOFT CROSSCOURT TO OPEN UP THE COURT

CHAPTER 8   Singles Practice Drills

PRACTICE DRILLS FOR THE SINGLES PLAYER

Success in sports is largely due to confidence. Confidence comes from knowing what you can and cannot do well in specific situations. The player who lacks confidence tries to do too much to the shot. The confident player plays within his or her capabilities. By specific and repetitious practice, you can build your strengths and improve your weaknesses. Building confidence in your own game increases your chances for success.

Anyone can learn the basic strokes of tennis well enough to begin playing and enjoying the game relatively quickly. However, the better you play, the more fun, challenging, and rewarding the game will be for you. If your aspirations are very high, be prepared to work for hours, months, and years to achieve your goals. Fortunately, most players believe that practicing tennis is basically fun. The purpose of this chapter is to give you concrete steps to follow in order to improve at the quickest possible rate.

Begin by isolating the game into three general areas of emphasis of practice, recognizing that there will be some overlap:

1. Backcourt Practice

2. Net Play Practice

3. Serve and Serve Return Practice

Next, proceed through the following three specific learning progressions in each area of practice:

1. Basic Groove Hitting: Balls tossed by a partner, ejected from a ball machine, or simply served and returned

2. Partner Rallies: Specifically definable sequences—an extension of basic groove hitting

3. Game Situations: Returning a random variation of shots both when you have little control over the type and timing of the situations that develop and when you try to control the situation that evolves

HINT: The purposes of all Basic Groove Hitting and Partner Rally drills are to isolate particular skills and, by constant repetition in a non-stress situation, give the player chances to develop confidence in hitting the shot or combination of shots.

MOVING PRACTICE WITH A BALL MACHINE

MOVING PRACTICE WITH A BALL MACHINE

BALL MACHINE OSCILLATION DRILL: BALLS 1 AND 3

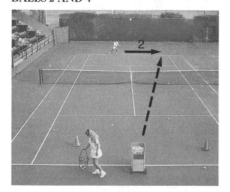

BALL MACHINE OSCILLATION DRILL: BALLS 2 AND 4

BACKCOURT PRACTICE

Basic Groove Hitting

1. *Moving to the Ball.* With the help of a tossing partner or a ball machine, practice returning wide balls. **Turn,** by stepping and jogging or running to where the ball will be *before* the ball gets there. (Try to beat the ball to the spot.) Emphasize adjusting your feet just before you step into the ball. **Recover,** by dropping your rear foot back toward the center of the court and then sliding back to your starting point. Practice forehands, then backhands; then, alternate short balls and deep balls. REMEMBER: Take your racket back with your first step, and **hold and correct** your finish.

CHALLENGES

Always have a target to which to hit. How many of ten balls can the tosser catch? How many of ten shots land in the targeted court area?

---

2. *Oscillation Drill.* Practicing running wide for alternating forehands and backhands is called "oscillation." Although oscillation may be done with tossed balls, it is one of the most relevant basic groove hitting drills for the ball machine. (Ten minutes of daily groundstroke grooving oscillation on the ball machine as a warm-up will benefit any player.) The following points are important to achieve the maximum benefit from ball machine oscillation:
   a. Always take the racket well back toward the ready-to-hit position with the first step you take.
   b. Be well on your way to the general area the ball will be coming to *before* the ball is ejected from the machine. This allows you to get to the ball in time to adjust your feet properly so that you can transfer your weight directly into your shot. A primary advantage of the ball machine is that you know where the ball is going to go. You can prepare for your shot well in advance and will know whether your preparation has been correct. *Never* wait until the ball is ejected and then try to run after it.
   c. **Hold** for a count or two after hitting the ball to make certain your finish is correct and that you are balanced. Make any necessary corrections, although it may mean you don't have time to hit the next shot. Until your swing becomes well grooved, it is important to have the ball ejection interval set to allow plenty of time between shots to **correct.**
   d. **Recover** to your set position by dropping your rear foot back toward the center of the court and sliding back. You have ample time to prepare for the next shot by immediately pushing off the inside foot and running to where the next ball will be.
   e. The general emphasis is on a *smooth and relaxed rhythm.* The entire side-to-side cycle is continuous, except for the brief **hold and correct** after each shot. Remember, you should not rush, so the time interval between shots is important.
   f. When working out with a partner, the hitter and retriever switch places when the retriever has picked up a full hopper of balls.

CHALLENGE

Always use a target (racket cover, cone, etc.). Aim for one target until you hit it, then aim for the other. REMEMBER: Control is more important than power.

Partner Rallies

With the help of a hitting partner, do the following practice rally drills:

1. *Rally Forehand to Forehand, Backhand to Backhand, Forehand to Backhand, and Backhand to Forehand.* Begin in the service court with a forehand and move back to full court as your control improves. Gradually emphasize depth, so that all balls land beyond the service line. Return to the center of the court after each shot. *IMPORTANT:* **Hold** *your finish (and* **correct** *if necessary) until the ball lands on the other side of the net. This prevents you from rushing your shots in practice.*

> ### CHALLENGE
>
> Hit ten balls without a miss, then proceed to the next drill. Increase to twenty hits without a miss.

2. *Crosscourt and Down-the-Line Rallies.* Player A hits only crosscourt shots; player B hits only down the line. *HINT:* Begin in the service court and gradually move to the backcourt. Hit three-quarter speed, and try not to hit too close to the line. (The emphasis is on keeping the rally going as long as possible.) When you are hurried, put more arc on your return. As you improve, try to keep the ball deep (beyond the service line).

> ### CHALLENGE
>
> How many successive balls can you and your partner keep in play that (1) land on the proper side of the court and (2) also land beyond the service line?

3. *Four-Hit Passing Shot Drill.* The net player (player A) is at the net on one side of the court with a bucket of balls. The player begins a four-hit cycle by putting the ball in play down the line (1). Player B returns the ball to the net player (2), who then volleys the ball crosscourt (3). Player B then runs over and hits the passing shot down the line (4). The cycle begins again as player A quickly puts another ball in play down the line.

   The cycle can be repeated by having player A hit the first ball crosscourt, in which case player B will end up hitting a crosscourt passing shot on the fourth ball.

   Player A then can move to the other side of the court to repeat both cycles. Remember, the second ball is always returned to the net player.

FOUR-HIT PASSING SHOT DRILL

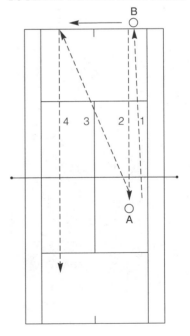

Game Situations

The following drills have no pattern:

1. *Playing Backcourt Points.* The purpose of this drill is to develop confidence and consistency when playing from the backcourt.

   Use a forehand to start the rally. (Two beginners may play "short court" by using the service squares as the rally target area.)

CHALLENGES

1. Play until one player wins seven points. *HINT:* Concentrate on being steady and accurate.

2. As a variation of the above, play until one player makes "two more errors than placements." Play rally points, with each of your errors counting as "minus 1" and each of your placements counting as "plus 1." You lose the game if you commit two more errors than placements before your opponent does. If one player gets pulled to the net, he or she should hit defensive volleys only. Emphasize changing pace, changing direction, and changing spin.

---

2. *Emphasizing the Approach Shot.*
   a. Begin a backcourt point and come to the net on the first short ball. The purpose of this drill is to learn to create and recognize opportunities to get to the net.

CHALLENGE

Play until one player wins seven points or until one player makes two more errors than placements.

CROSSCOURT RALLY UNTIL SHORT BALL; THEN ATTACK DOWN THE LINE

b. Begin with a crosscourt rally with both players in the backcourt. When a short ball is hit to you, move in and hit the approach shot down the line. The backcourt player tries to pass you. The purpose of this drill is to develop a good approach shot as well as confidence in hitting a solid passing shot.

CHALLENGE

Play until one player wins seven points or until one player makes two more errors than placements.

3. *Emphasizing the Passing Shot.*

   a. *Three-on-one passing shot drill.* The purpose of this drill is to develop a good approach shot as well as confidence in hitting a solid passing shot. Player A hits ball (1) to player D's backhand and comes to the net. Player D hits the passing shot (2). Player A then volleys the ball to the other side of the court (3). Player B repeats player A's pattern. After several cycles, players A, B, and C direct the first ball to player D's forehand. Finally, players A, B, and C alternate hitting the first ball to player D's forehand and backhand.

THREE-ON-ONE PASSING SHOT DRILL

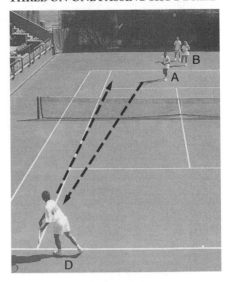

CHALLENGE

When player D makes two errors, he or she goes to the other side, and all players rotate. Which player can play the most consecutive points before making a passing shot error?

---

   b. *Instructor feeds the short ball.* The purpose of this drill is to develop consistency on the passing shot, without knowing ahead of time where the approach shot will be hit. The instructor stands at the net post just off the court and feeds a short ball to one of the backcourt players (player A or B). This player hits an approach shot and comes to the net. The opponent tries to pass or lob to win the point.

INSTRUCTOR FEEDS SHORT BALL

CHALLENGE

Player C or D replaces partner on his or her side of the net when that player makes an error. Without making an error, how many successive points can be played by the player attempting the passing shot?

---

   c. *One up, one back.* The purpose of this drill is to develop confidence in hitting passing shots when on the run and when tired. Player A is at net on one side of the court. Player B starts at the backcourt. Player B returns all balls to player A's side of the court. Player A volleys them back to just barely within reach of B. The object is to make player B run as much as possible for each ball while keeping the ball in play for as long as possible.

ONE UP, ONE BACK

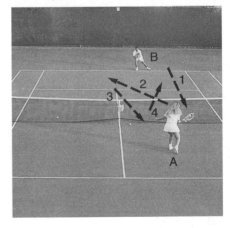

CHALLENGE

Use only ten balls. See how long they last before switching players A and B.

OSCILLATION VOLLEY DRILL

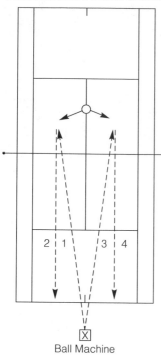

Ball Machine

THREE-HIT APPROACH SHOT DRILL

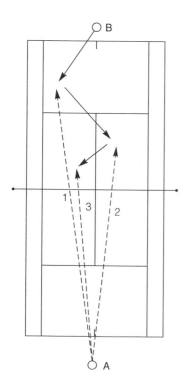

NET PLAY PRACTICE

Basic Groove Hitting

1. *Volleys*. With the help of a tossing partner or use of a ball machine, practice:
    a. Forehands, then backhands
    b. Low forehands, then low backhands
    c. Wide forehands, then wide backhands

HINT: Move diagonally forward to the volley and always recover back to your home base after each shot.

2. *Oscillation Volley Drill*. Practice returning alternating forehand and backhand volleys. This may be done with tossed balls or a ball machine.
    a. Practice normal, waist-high balls
    b. Practice low volleys (move back a little in the service square, perhaps almost to the center **T**)

HINT: Especially on the wide and low volleys, it is critically important to move diagonally forward to the volley. (Stepping first with the outside foot helps to in-still this habit.) Also, for the low volley, emphasize bending from the knees and not from the waist.

> **CHALLENGES**
>
> How many of ten balls can you return that your partner can catch for both the regular volley and the oscillation volley? If using a ball machine, how many of ten balls can you hit to near targets placed at various places on the court?

3. *Three-Hit Cycle (Approach–Volley–Volley)*. Player A feeds three shots to the other side—(1) a short ball, (2) a wide volley, and (3) a wide volley. Player B, beginning at the baseline, hits a forehand approach shot and moves toward the net. Player B then hits a backhand first volley and moves closer to the net to put away a forehand volley. Player B then returns to the back of the line. Player C repeats the three-hit cycle, but begins with a backhand approach shot, follows with a forehand first volley, and ends with a backhand volley. This drill may also be done using a ball machine.

HINT: This drill affords extra practice on the approach shot, but even more espe-cially, it is a good drill for the player to work on a quick split after the approach, followed by developing the feeling of closing in toward the net on the second volley.

> **CHALLENGE**
>
> How many successive times can you make all three shots? (Use targets to develop confidence in hitting a deep approach shot down the line, a deep first volley from midcourt, and a short angle volley from your final position near the net.)

4. *Overheads*. Tossed balls or machine.
    a. As the hitter develops more confidence and a good rhythm, use oscillation and deeper overheads. Gradually move into randomly directed overheads.

HINT: The hitter always returns to home base with a good split.

Partner Rallies

With the help of a hitting partner, do the following practice rally drills:

1. *Volley Wide Balls*. One player is at the backcourt and the other at the net. Use only one side of the court and return to the center mark each time. The volleyer hits forehand volleys only, and only to the backcourt player's backhand, or vice versa.

   CHALLENGE

   How long can you keep the ball in play?

2. *Oscillation Volleys (Crosscourt, Down-the-Line)*. The backcourt player hits only down the line, and the volleyer hits only crosscourt. Keep the ball in play rather than trying to win the point.

   CHALLENGE

   How long can you keep the ball in play?

3. *Quick Volleys*. Both players are at the net and volley either straight ahead to each other or, standing slightly off-center, diagonally across the court.

   HINT: Start with just forehands or backhands. Emphasize keeping the ball in play and good footwork. As you get better, speed up the balls and hit to either side.

   CHALLENGES

   How long can you keep the ball in play? How many rallies can you "win"?

4. *Net Approach Practice*. The purpose of this drill is to work on the timing of the split as well as on developing hand-eye speed. Both players begin just in front of the baseline. With each shot, both move forward a couple of steps. By the third or fourth shot, both partners are at net in a continuous quick volley rally.

   HINT: Be certain to use a split, landing on the balls of your feet with each volley your partner hits. Do not rush your approach—stay balanced and under control.

WIDE VOLLEY DRILL

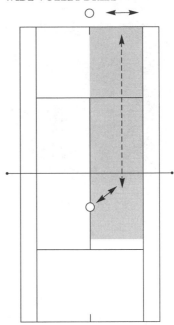

OSCILLATION VOLLEYS

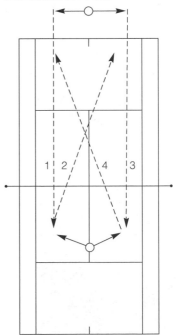

NET APPROACH

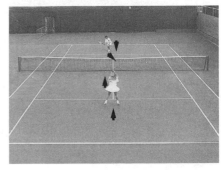

SINGLE-FILE APPROACH VOLLEY DRILL

5. *Single-File Volley Approach Drill.* This drill also affords work on the timing of the split. A player or an instructor is on one side of the net, and four or five players are on the other side, just behind the service line in a single-file line. Player A moves in and splits just as the instructor volleys the ball. Player A then steps forward to return the volley to the instructor and goes to the back of the line as player B moves in to repeat the process. Use only one ball.

HINT: Don't volley too hard. In fact, volley slightly "up." Concentrate on a good split and on moving forward into the volley. It is important for player B and then player C to follow closely behind the volleyer.

> **CHALLENGE**
>
> How many balls can your group keep in play without a miss? If several courts are doing this drill simultaneously, which court can keep the ball in play the longest?

TO PRACTICE BACKHAND LOBS, PLAY DIAGONALLY IN AD COURT

6. *Practice Overheads.* (Player A is in the backcourt; player B is at the net.)
   a. Player A lobs and player B returns with an overhead. The net player always returns to home base with a split after each shot.

HINT: This is a good chance for the backcourt partner to work on lobbing. Be certain to move the feet on the lob and to follow through the shot. Try to lob fairly high and deep. Player B should work more on placement than on power. Try using the center of the court, then move over to hit diagonally to each other. (This gives the player hitting lobs a good chance to work on lobbing from his or her weak side—for example, if the partners are in the ad court, the lobs will be mostly backhand lobs.)

> **CHALLENGE**
>
> How many balls can you keep in play?

UP AND BACK DRILL

   b. *Up and Back Drill.* The purpose of this drill is to give the backcourt player experience in hitting deep, defensive lobs, and yet still be able to play aggressively while returning the partner's overhead. Player A alternates drives and lobs; player B alternates volleys and overheads, moving "up" for the volley and "back" for the overhead. Play some down the middle, then diagonally.

HINT: Use high and deep lobs to get partner away from the net. Always return player B's overhead with a hard drive, even though it should be directed right back to player B. Player B returns all balls back to player A and recovers quickly back to the net after each overhead. The overhead may also be played aggressively.

> **CHALLENGE**
>
> How many balls can you keep in play?

Game Situations

The following drills have no pattern:

1. *Up and Back Points.* This drill is similar to the Up and Back Drill in the preceeding Partner Rallies section. However, no specific hitting pattern is followed. This drill teaches the net player the importance of a quick recovery after the overhead, as well as the importance of a deep volley when hitting from midcourt. It also gives the backcourt player experience in opening up the forecourt by using the lob. Player A is in the backcourt on one side of the court, and player B is at the net diagonally opposite player A. Both players try to win the point: player A by using a combination of lobs and drives, player B by using overheads and volleys.

HINTS: If both players need work on backhand volleys or lobs, use the ad court, or vice versa. Player A should use lobs at least every second or third shot.

CHALLENGE

Play until one player wins seven points, then change positions.

---

2. *Australian Two-on-One.*
   a. *Two up at the net, one in the backcourt.* The purpose of this drill is to force quick recoveries by the backcourt player, and to learn to "stay with" the passing shot when extended fully on the run and when tired. The net players try to keep the ball in play so that the backcourt player can just barely get to each ball.

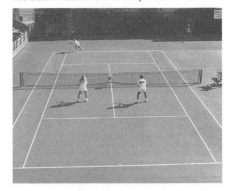

AUSSIE DRILL: TWO UP, ONE BACK

HINT: The backcourt player should not overhit, but should try to make each shot simulate a passing shot, thus keeping all balls out of the middle. Take any short ball early and aggressively.

CHALLENGE

See how long the backcourt player can keep going. (It is difficult to hit good shots when really tired.)

AUSSIE DRILL: TWO BACK, ONE UP

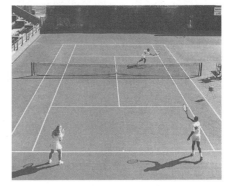

   b. *Two back at the baseline, one up.* The purpose of this drill is to teach the net player (1) to recover quickly, (2) the liability of the short volley, and (3) confidence in the range of motion at the net. Two players are in the backcourt and only one is at the net. The object is for the backcourt players to move the net player around as much as possible, but the net player should be able to reach every ball.

HINT: The backcourt players should use many lobs and should mix in some soft passing shots as well.

CHALLENGE

How long can the net player keep going?

**SCRAMBLE DRILL: RETURN ALL
BALLS AWAY FROM FEEDER (B)**

3. *The "Scramble."* The purposes of this drill are to increase confidence, speed, and agility when at the net as well as to improve conditioning. Player A serves and comes to the net. Player B, who has a bucket of balls, disregards the balls hit by player A and, instead, uses balls from the bucket to feed net player A one shot after another for approximately a twelve-shot sequence. The object is to make player A hit the first volley and move quickly from side to side and up and back for hard drives, lobs, and soft balls. A variation is for player B to start by moving player A from side to side in the backcourt and then to feed a short ball so that player A can work on an approach to the net off the ground rather than off the serve. All balls should be returned to the opposite side of the court from the feeder (player B).

HINT: The feeder must be very cognizant of any loose balls on the court. Make each turn a "quality" turn—use deep lobs and wide balls, especially when feeding the first volley.

CHALLENGE

How many twelve-shot turns can be completed with the net rusher not missing a ball?

SERVE AND SERVE RETURN PRACTICE

Basic Groove Hitting

Always keep in mind the great importance of practicing all types of serves and returns to all parts of the court. (When one player is practicing the serve, the other player can be practicing the return.)

1. *The Serve.* A player is only as good as his or her second serve in pressure situations. When practicing your serve, spend most of your time trying to make your second serve stronger, instead of attempting to make your first serve harder.

> ### CHALLENGE
>
> After a good serve warm-up, serve fifteen serves each to targets placed (1) wide in the deuce court, (2) the center T of the deuce court, (3) the center T of the ad court, and (4) wide to the ad court.

2. *The Return.* Practice your returns from different depths relative to your home base on the baseline, and practice different kinds of returns—the basic drive, the underspin, etc. Remember to cut off the angle on any wide serves.

> ### CHALLENGE
>
> How many balls in succession can you return down the line? Crosscourt? Short? Deep? (Use targets.)

3. *Serve and Volley, Return and Pass Shot: Four-Hit Drill.* The server should work on developing a good serve-and-volley rhythm, emphasizing a precise and balanced split and a diagonally forward movement to the volley. The receiver must practice stepping into the return and staying forward as opposed to pulling up or back on the passing shot. (1) Player A serves to the deuce court. (2) Player B returns the ball down the middle. (3) Player A (server) volleys to the ad court. (4) Player B then goes for the passing shot. The sequence is repeated, except player A serves the next ball to the ad court. Player B then returns from the ad court and passes from the deuce court.

> ### CHALLENGE
>
> How many times can you repeat the entire four-shot sequence?

Partner Rallies

With the help of a hitting partner, do the following practice rally drills:

1. *Two-on-One Serve and Volley.* Players A and B alternate serves and volleys. Player C returns. The server should emphasize second serves. The receiver should work on only one type of return at a time, such as a chip or drive, standing back or standing in close, etc.

> ### CHALLENGE
>
> The server announces where the serve and first volley will be hit; the receiver points to where the return will be hit. When the receiver makes two errors, one of the servers switches sides and becomes the new receiver.

FOUR-HIT SERVE AND VOLLEY DRILL

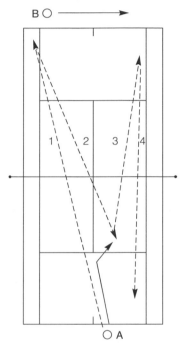

TWO-ON-ONE SERVE AND VOLLEY

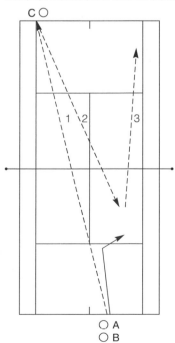

Game Situations

The following drills have no pattern:

1. *King of the Court.* The purpose of this drill is to "mix" players on the team or in the class, as well as to teach confidence in the serve-and-volley game. (This is a great game for an odd number of players on one or several courts. The "winner" stays on; the "loser" drops out; the "challenger" serves.)

> **CHALLENGE**
>
> Scoring options:
>
> 1. Play serve-and-volley points to seven.
> 2. Serve until one player makes two errors.
> 3. Play serve-and-volley points until one player makes two more errors than placements.
> 4. Each player keeps track of the total number of "wins."

BUMPER TENNIS

2. *Bumper Tennis.* This is a great drill to "mix" different ability levels, or to quickly set up a fairly accurate team/class ranking. (In this case, it is not necessary to have the server serve and volley each point.) If there are five to seven players assigned to each court, the two high point winners move "up," the two low point winners move "down," and the middle players stay on the same court for another rotation. (If there is a great disparity in abilities, it sometimes helps to have a mandatory "drop out" when one player wins three points in succession.)

> **CHALLENGE**
>
> Play points (backcourt only, serve-and-volley, or "anything goes"). The winner of the point stays on the court to be challenged by the next player in line (*NOTE:* Maximum number of three successive wins). The two top point winners move up one court, and two low point players move down a court. The object is to end up on the number-one court at the end of the drill period (30–45 minutes). Each mini-rotation lasts 10–12 minutes.

3. *Serve Return: Playing with a Plan.* The purposes of this drill are to teach the receiver to play the return game with a definite plan in mind and to increase confidence in his or her ability to execute this plan. (This helps to force the receiver out of his or her normal "comfort zone.") The server must serve and volley on first serves but may serve and volley on second serves. The receiver should adopt a specific "theme" for each service game. For example:
   a. Direct all returns to a specific volley.
   b. Assume different receiving "home bases."
   c. Drive return followed by a lob.
   d. On all second serves, either take the return early and get to net, or run around and hit a forehand.

> **CHALLENGE**
>
> One player serves for four successive games or until he or she loses the serve. Then the server and receiver switch places. How many times can the receiver prevent the server from winning four successive games?

CHAPTER 9   Advanced Doubles Strategy

As the basic doubles situations presented in Chapter 5 become more familiar, the novice begins to realize that doubles is an exciting and fast-moving game requiring great teamwork and communication between partners. Keep those requirements in mind when choosing a partner. Also, try to choose a partner whose style of play complements your own. (A quick "touch" player and a more powerful partner often make a good team.)

Although the court in doubles play is 9 feet wider than in singles, two players can cover the entire area with comparative ease. Unlike singles, when you are hitting from the backcourt, the probability is decreased that you will maneuver your opponents out of position; the angle to which to hit is just too limited. You are also unlikely to use power as effectively from the backcourt, since from that position it is difficult to hit "through" two net players.

STRATEGY FOR THE SERVING TEAM

Who Should Serve First?

Usually the best server should serve first in every set. Sometimes a special playing condition such as wind at the server's back, absence of sun glare, or a very good and active partner at the net will favor beginning with the weaker server. (Neither server should ever have to serve into the sun if one is left-handed and one is right-handed.)

Why the First Serve Is So Important

In doubles, fewer chances should be taken with the first serve than are taken in singles, and more margin should be allowed (more spin, for example) to get the ball in play. A consistent first serve is important for three reasons: (1) The partner at the net can poach more effectively. (2) The server can come to the net more readily. An intermediate player should come to net on many first serves but much less often on second serves. An advanced player will come to net on both serves, since the majority of points can be won by the team who gets to the net first. (3) The server has the strategic advantage. If the first serve is missed, however, the receiver will probably have an easier return on the second serve. (The second serve is usually hit with more safety and spin, which gives it a tendency to land short.) You can take fewer chances on the second serve, and the receiver knows it will probably be served to his or her backhand. Thus the receiver can gamble—run around his or her backhand, move in closer and quicker, hit harder, and so on. A short second serve lets the receiver join his or her partner at the net more easily.

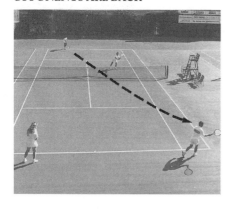

SERVE WIDE WHEN BOTH OPPONENTS ARE BACK

Considerations on When to Serve Wide

The most effective wide serves are the slice to the forehand in the deuce court and the twist to the backhand in the ad court. The *wide serve* can be effective when (1) your opponent is getting to the net off the return too quickly (a wide serve slows your opponent down by moving him or her wide for the return); (2) your opponent has trouble returning a wide shot; or (3) both opponents are behind the baseline. This tends to pull the receiver wide, opening up the court for the poach by the server's partner, or opening up the middle of the court for the server's first volley.

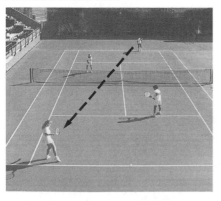

SERVE IN TIGHT TO CRAMP THE FOREHAND RETURN

Considerations on When to Serve Down the Middle

The serve to the middle of the court in the *deuce court* is effective when served to the backhand. The ball served to the center of the court makes it easier for the server's partner to poach toward the center since it is more difficult for the opponent to return the ball to the alley with significant angle. For this reason, in the deuce court the server's partner at the net will often begin the point standing closer to the center of the court, since the basic serve is to the backhand (middle of the court). In the ad court, the serve will probably be wider, so the partner often stands closer to the alley.

Serve down the middle to the *ad court* when (1) your opponent is "keying" for the usual serve to the backhand, especially on an ad point; (2) your opponent overswings regularly on the forehand return (this ball can be served in tight to cramp the swing); or (3) the receiver has a good wide return.

In either the deuce court or the ad court, a serve in tight to the body is good, especially on a second serve, since the receiver has little room to do much to the return.

The Poach

Poaching is a strategy in which the net player moves toward his or her partner's side of the court to intercept a return shot. The net player should always move diagonally forward on the poach to take the ball as close to the net as possible. The poaching net player aims the return shot at the opening between the receiver (who is back) and the net player, or slightly toward the net player's feet. If the poaching player's momentum carries him or her to the server's side of the court, the serving partner moves over to cover the poacher's original side. If both members of the receiving team are in the backcourt, the poach may be directed at either player, down the middle, or to the short angle.

If you are the server on a team that poaches often, you might serve from a position closer to the center of the court. In order to protect against the angle return, serve more down the middle. The poach stands the best chance of being effective on the first serve, so concentrate on getting the first serve in and don't try a risky serve.

The poach is a good move in the following situations: (1) You are having trouble winning the point while serving to a particular side of the court. In this case the poach can break the receiver's rhythm and keep the receiver from grooving the return. A poaching net player gives the receiver many more things to think about. (2) The point is a big one, such as ad out. Here the poach can help the server out of a jam, especially if the server has had to struggle to win serve. (3) The serve is deep. If the ball lands near the service line, be ready to move. (4) The return is a floating underspin. This shot often lends itself to poaching, since the ball is rising.

Poach Signals. When the serving team decides to poach often, the net player should "signal" any intentions to his or her partner. For example, a closed fist means "stay" (often used with a fake poach), and an open hand means "go." The thumb or a finger can point out the direction of the serve. You might think of the net player as the catcher in baseball, who is calling the pitches for the pitcher—the server. Like the pitcher, the server must feel comfortable with the call and can verbally "call off" any signal he or she does not like.

The server must *always* verbally acknowledge that he or she has seen the signal. If the server agrees with the call, the decision to poach becomes an all-or-nothing commitment. Immediately after hitting the serve, the server must cross over to cover the opposite alley.

Signals are also used to dictate where the ball is to be served. As a result, the server's partner assumes home base position well away from the alley at about the center of the service square. If the signal is for a wide serve, the net player has ample time to move to the alley to protect against a down-the-line return. More important, by starting from a position closer to the center of the court, the net player has greatly increased his or her ability to cover more court when poaching.

STAY	GO
SERVE INTO BODY	**SERVE INTO BODY**

SERVE WIDE RIGHT	**SERVE WIDE RIGHT**

SERVE WIDE LEFT	**SERVE WIDE LEFT**

AUSTRALIAN DOUBLES POSITIONS

AUSTRALIAN DOUBLES POSITIONS

Play "Australian" Doubles

Another service strategy to counteract an effective return (specifically the wide crosscourt return on the backhand from the ad court) is for the server's partner to get positioned on the same side of the court as the server, where the crosscourt return can be intercepted. The serve must be made from close to the center of the court so the server can move over to the opposite side to cover the territory usually covered by his or her partner.

If the serve is to the ad court, the net player starts at the net on the left (instead of the right) side of the court, near the center service line. The serve is made from near the center on the left side, and the server moves to the right side to continue the point. The receiver is forced to return down the line, which is often difficult for the player with a good crosscourt backhand. The maneuver may be tried on certain points to break the receiver's rhythm or to help get out of a particular jam.

The net player may decide to poach from the "center-of-the-court position." In this case, the net player should give the poach signal to the server.

If the server has an especially good volley on one side or is weak on the other, a team may use Australian doubles. For example, if Australian doubles is used when serving to the ad court, the server should rarely have to hit a backhand volley, since the server will be moving toward the forehand side of the court.

Try the Australian formation early in a match in which your team is comfortably ahead in a game (30-15, 40-0). Serve to the backhand. (The server's partner should not poach at first since the serving team is just testing to see how well the receiver can return with a backhand down the line.) Remember how your opponent reacts. If the return is tentative and unsure, use the Australian formation any time you are in trouble (behind) in a game, until your opponent proves that he or she can return well down the line. If your opponent is aggressive on the return, however, you will use Australian more to change the receiver's rhythm than to get out of trouble.

Australian doubles is not often used on a second serve, since the receiver will anticipate a serve to the backhand and can run around it and hit a forehand at the maximum angle and therefore stands a good chance of winning the point.

"MONSTER" DOUBLES POSITIONS

Play "Monster" Doubles

In "monster" doubles (a variation of Australian doubles), the server always serves from close to the center service line. The server's partner straddles the center service line just a step or two inside the service square. Serves are directed into the body or to the center T, affording the receiver minimum angle on the return. Therefore, the net player has to signal only the direction he or she is going to move.

Since both partners start essentially in the center of the court, both players must move toward opposite alleys when the ball is served. This move can confuse a good receiving team. More important, a player who is having trouble holding serve can be helped because the net player has more freedom to move in either direction. A net player who is very quick and has good hands may be able to intercept more balls when moving from the monster position. Or, depending on which way the players move, monster doubles is a good way to cover up a weak forehand or backhand volley. The mentality of the net player is "I want that ball!"

Playing Against "Monster" Doubles. Don't become too worried about the net player's movements. Concentrate on returning to one side, usually down the line, until the return has proven ineffective. Occasionally, try a down-the-middle return, since both players will be moving away from the middle of the court. If the poacher is effectively intercepting many balls, both partners on the receiving team should move back behind the baseline. When both members of the receiving team are in the backcourt, it is not so critical to hit the return low and away from the net player.

STRATEGY FOR THE RECEIVING TEAM

Who Returns from Which Court?

In determining which partner receives from the deuce court and which from the ad court, the prime consideration should be, Where does each receiver feel more comfortable? Usually a player with a natural underspin backhand will play the deuce (forehand) court, where most serves tend to be in close to the receiver's backhand. The partner with the better drive backhand (topspin) usually plays the ad (backhand) court, since there is more room on this side for a fuller return swing.

Other factors should be considered as well. A left-handed player might play the ad court expecting that most serves will be directed to the backhands (or down the middle) and to keep both partners' forehands on the outside, where more reach is needed. Or the left-hander might play the deuce court to keep both forehands in the middle, where most balls are hit.

The stronger player might play the deuce court, where more points (at least half) are served (for example, the ad receiver returns one less point in a 40-15 game). The player who is better able to handle the pressure at "game" point may play the ad court.

Hitting the Return

A good return of serve is one of the most important shots in doubles, because it sets the tempo of the point. In advanced doubles the receiver assumes that the server is coming to the net, so the receiver's goal is to keep the ball low to the approaching server in order to make the server volley up. On the return of serve, the receiver also often comes to the net, especially on return of second serves, although the first rule is get the ball in play.

As receiver you should adjust your court position so you have the best chance to get the ball in play. For example, move back a little from the baseline if you are having difficulty returning a hard serve. The farther back you stand, the more you can swing and drive the return with topspin. (However, since you sacrifice being closer to the net, it will be almost impossible to get to net behind your return. Your opponents will have more time to poach as well.) The closer in you stand, the more you must shorten your swing and block or chip the return (more underspin). Also, you have a better chance to protect against the poach, to hit down on the return, and to move in to the net to volley.

If a team is known to poach often, start the match by hitting behind the poacher early so your opponents will know that you are not afraid to do so. You might also try to chip lob return off a second serve to get the ball over the net player's head. If that doesn't work, start the point with both partners on the baseline; the poacher has less chance to be effective because the target is reduced.

Against Australian doubles, the basic play is to take the ball early and hit aggressively down the line. If you have difficulty doing this, move your partner from the net to the backcourt with you. If the serving team plays Australian on their second serve, the ball will probably be served to your backhand, so run around it and crack a forehand return.

The Receiver's Partner

If you are the receiver's partner, you normally begin on the center of the service line. Your responsibility is to call the "out" serves and watch your partner's return. If the return is reasonably low and to the approaching server, move forward into a position about 10 feet from the net. If the return of serve is low and to the center of the court, take a step forward and then you can poach to the center. (Be certain to move diagonally forward any time you poach.) If the return goes toward the net player (either because of a poor return or a poach) move back and toward the center to give yourself time to react and to cut off the opening in the middle of the court.

MOVE BACK SOME IF YOU ARE HAVING TROUBLE WITH YOUR RETURN

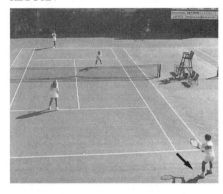

THE RECEIVER'S PARTNER HELPS TO CALL "OUT" SERVES.

WHEN BOTH PARTNERS ARE BACK, STAND SEVERAL FEET BEHIND THE BASELINE

WHEN BOTH PARTNERS ARE BACK, STAND SEVERAL FEET BEHIND THE BASELINE

When Both Partners Are in the Backcourt

As the receiver's partner, you might choose to stand back at the baseline at these times: (1) The server's partner is poaching often (on first serves, for example) and effectively. The poacher is less able to hit an outright winner (at your feet or between partners) if you are back. (2) Your partner is having particular trouble with the return. With both partners back, the receiver has more margin—the low return is not so critical and the receiver can concentrate more on just getting the ball back. (3) The server is consistently beating the receiver to the net and by better positioning is winning the point on the first volley. (Play from the backcourt requires a less exacting return and makes it more difficult for the opposing server to put the first volley away for the winner.) (4) The serving team is a "groove" team and has established a fast pace and momentum. The receiving team should stay back and try to break the momentum. This can be an effective psychological maneuver on select points, such as the first two points of a game, if the serving team has easily held serve in the first part of the set. (5) You want to exploit an opponent's weak overhead or the weaker partner. In this situation, the receiver and partner stand substantially back and only try to get the ball in play on the return. Once it is in play, try to keep hitting to the weaker player. If that player is at the net, alternate lobs with aggressive topspin drives to make that player move up and back. (If the ball is returned short to you or if the ball bounces behind the net players, both you and your partner can take the offense by moving in to the net.)

Since both partners are in the backcourt, the net players should be expecting the lob. Therefore, don't use a low percentage topspin lob, which is most effective in an unexpected situation. Instead, use a high, defensive lob to force the opponents to hit from deep in their court.

Be Patient.   Don't make the mistake of trying to overpower your opponents at the net. Be patient and try to keep the up–back (drive–lob) combination rally going until the volley or overhead is returned short enough for you to effectively hit hard in an attempt to win the point outright.

PLAYER B LOOKS TO POACH IF THE BALL IS KEPT LOW

PLAYER B LOOKS TO POACH IF THE BALL IS KEPT LOW

When One Partner Is at the Net and the Other Back

Often the receiver cannot get to the net to join his or her partner after the return. In that case, player B is vulnerable. However, player B remains at the net in case his or her partner (A) is able to return the ball low. If that happens, player B should be ready to move in and cut the ball off (a poach), since the opposing net player (C or D) will be volleying up.

However, if player A lobs, then net player B retreats back toward the baseline, primarily to avoid injury by the opposing team's overhead smash, but also to have a little more time to react to the shot. Net player B tries to get back all the way behind the baseline, but no matter where he or she is located when the opponent hits the ball, the net player should stop and "set" to have a chance to react. It is important to realize that a backcourt player will most likely lob when both opponents are at the net, and the net player should be ready to move back at the instant his or her partner hits the lob, especially if the partner is returning from a position deep in the court. (One reason the net player always watches the ball except when his or her partner is serving is so that the lob can be recognized immediately and the net player will have more time to move back.)

When both partners are at the net, the opponents should direct most drives down the middle so the net players are forced to volley with little angle. A lob may be hit to either partner to get that player away from the net and to open up some room in the forecourt for the next drive.

When Both Teams Are at the Net

Points in advanced doubles often end with all four players at the net, like in-fighting in boxing. While both teams wait for an offensive opportunity, the emphasis is on keeping the ball low. Softer shots are often required. As soon as one team hits the ball up, the opposing team moves in for the knockout punch and volleys down.

Which Partner Is Responsible for Which Ball? In order to avoid opening up any unnecessary angles, most balls are hit down the middle when all four players are at the net. If you are moving in when a ball is returned down the middle, you should probably take the ball. If you have been pulled wide, your partner must move over and cover the middle. If your opponents are returning the wide ball, the partner on that side must cover the alley while the other partner covers the center. If neither player is moving, the player with the forehand in the middle will usually take the shot. If there is any doubt, go for the ball. Above all, don't be indecisive.

The Importance of Keeping the Ball Low. Return the low ball to the feet of the player farthest from you. The crosscourt volley gives the ball more time to drop to your opponent's feet since it passes over the lower part of the net. If you are successful in returning low, move in close, because your opponent must volley up and you will be in a good position to volley down for the winner. Be aggressive and keep attacking. The farther back you stand, the easier it is for your opponents to hit to your feet. Try an extreme angle shot only if you can probably hit an outright winner. (Don't give your opponents an even greater angle for their return.)

What to Do When the Ball Is Returned High. If the ball is returned up to you, move in quickly and hit down at the feet of the opponent nearer to you. Anticipate the high ball by virtue of your low return. Begin closing in before your opponent hits the return. The partner who is not hitting should be ready to back up the hitting player in case the opponents try a quick lob or lob volley. (The lob volley is a difficult shot, however, and will not often be successful.)

MOVE IN CLOSE AFTER A LOW RETURN

When Both Partners Are at the Net and the Opponents Are Back

Be Patient. Realize that the rallies will be longer and it will be harder to put the ball away. Don't try to power the ball past your opponents. Short, angled volleys can be effective, since they tend to pull one partner up and out of position. But if you don't have enough angle to win the point outright, keep the ball deep and down the middle. This will keep your opponents back on defense and confuse them a little about who will return the ball.

Expect the Lob. Play farther from the net. Fifteen feet from the net is not too far back for your home-base set position, especially if you are not too confident in your overhead. Try to hit every ball *before* it bounces. (Only an extremely high and short lob should be allowed to bounce.)

If a lob goes over your head, you have very little chance to win the point. However, your partner should cross diagonally back from the net and try to return it with a high, defensive lob. (Your opponents will be coming to the net if a ball is lobbed over your head.) You should also move to the backcourt and cross over to your partner's original side of the court.

If you are hitting the overhead from deep in your court, hit with more spin and less power, and hit it more down the middle. Smash all short lobs and high balls hard and down the middle unless you have enough angle to win the point outright. When both opponents are back, you have a great chance to play the weaker player.

YOUR OPPONENTS WILL BE COMING TO THE NET IF THE BALL IS LOBBED OVER YOUR HEAD

CHAPTER 10 Doubles Practice Drills

VOLLEY DRILLS WITH AN INSTRUCTOR

1. *Poaching*. The purpose of this drill is to help give players confidence in covering more court at net. Players stand single file in line 1, just behind the service line and a couple of feet inside the alley. Player A comes in toward the net and makes a split in the normal home base position. (Use chalk to mark the spot.) The instructor feeds a ball crosscourt, and player A moves diagonally forward toward the net to hit a forehand volley. Player A then goes to the other side of the court to form line 2. After all players in line 1 have hit forehand volleys, the drill is repeated from line 2 with backhand volleys.

2. *Six-Player Volley Rally*. The purpose of this drill is to help increase hand speed at the net. Three players are on one side of the net, and two additional players flank the instructor on the other side. The instructor has a bucket of balls and starts the rally by hitting the ball anywhere on the other side. The rally is played to completion, and the instructor quickly starts another rally.

3. *Keep Away*. The purpose of this drill is to increase the net player's confidence in his or her ability to cover the court. Six players are on the court—two at each baseline and two at the net opposite each other. The instructor starts the rally, and the point continues with the four backcourt players trying to keep the ball away from the net players.

SIX-PLAYER VOLLEY RALLY

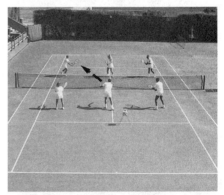

CHALLENGE

When a net player has won three points, that side of the net rotates clockwise one position.

KEEP AWAY

WORKUP DRILL

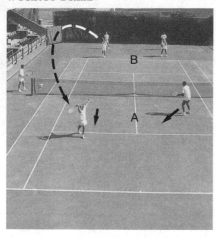

DROPOUT

TOUCH-SHOT DRILL

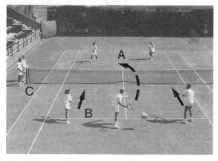

APPROACH DRILL

TEAMWORK DRILLS WITH AN INSTRUCTOR

1. *Doubles Workup*. This drill is designed to teach the backcourt team how to "work" the point when both opponents are at the net. Team A is at the net and team B is at the baseline. The instructor stands just off the side of the court at the net post and starts the point by "feeding" the ball to team B. When the point is over, team C replaces team B at the baseline, and the teams continue to alternate after each point.

HINT: Learn to use the lob to open up the forecourt, rather than trying to blast the ball through your opponents at net.

> ### CHALLENGE
>
> When one team loses three points, it is replaced by Team C.

2. *Doubles Dropout*. The object of this drill is to help develop quick hands and reactions. Both team A and team B start at the net. Team C is off the court at the net post. The instructor stands behind team B and feeds a volley to team A. The "point" continues to completion.

> ### CHALLENGE
>
> Team C replaces the first team to lose three points.

3. *Doubles Touch-Shot Drill*. This drill teaches the value of the soft, low shot to set up the next hit. Both teams start a couple of steps behind the service line. The instructor stands inside the baseline but behind team B. The instructor feeds a soft, low ball to team A, which tries to return it soft and low to team B, and then close in toward the net. Team B also closes in, but cannot move until just before team A hits its first shot. The point is played to completion, with both teams trying to keep the ball low in order to close in and hit down for a winner.

> ### CHALLENGE
>
> After one team wins three points, sides of the net are changed, and team C replaces the losing team.

4. *Doubles Approach*. This drill incorporates the approach shot (a groundstroke or volley) and teaches the value of keeping the ball low and both partners moving together. Both teams start on the baseline. The instructor, standing just outside the net post, feeds a short ball or a soft "blooper" to either team. That team then approaches the net, and the point is played to completion. (Remember, the backcourt team should play defensively, using many lobs to open up the short court.)

> ### CHALLENGE
>
> Team C replaces the first team to lose three points, and the "game" starts over. How many consecutive "games" can a team win?

DOUBLES DRILLS WITH ONLY TWO PLAYERS

1. *The Attack*. The purpose of this drill is to work on "closing in" to the net. (Players use only diagonally opposite sides of the court.) The server hits a second serve (one serve only) and comes to the net. The receiver returns and also comes in. Play full speed, and play the point to completion. Use soft, low volleys to force your opponent to volley up to you so you can move in and put the ball away. For the purposes of this drill, neither player may hit a lob volley.

HINT: If the receiver can (1) hit the return early and from well within the playing court, and (2) keep the return wide out into the alley, he or she has an excellent chance to win the point.

CHALLENGE

The "winner" is the first player to win seven points. When this happens, then the other player serves. How many seven-point games can you win?

2. *The Defense*. The purpose of this drill is to allow the receiver to practice staying in the backcourt and "working the point." The server both serves and volleys crosscourt. The receiver defends by staying back after the return, and "works" the point by mixing high, deep lobs and drives. (All balls must go diagonally crosscourt.)

CHALLENGE

How long can the receiver keep the ball in play?

PRACTICE GAMELIKE SITUATIONS

It is important not only to practice drills but also to practice in more gamelike situations, especially ones you will have to adopt in certain conditions and in certain matches. Practice the following situations as both the serving team and the receiving team.

1. *Serving Team*. (The server always serves and volleys.)
   a. *Using signals and poaching*.

HINT: The net player executes a pronounced body fake when not moving.

> **CHALLENGE**
>
> Play twelve-point tiebreakers, poaching on at least two of every three first serves and on half of the second serves.

   b. *Australian doubles*. Each player serves four points in the ad court using Australian doubles.

HINT: The net player should poach on at least one of the four serve points.

   c. *Monster doubles*.

> **CHALLENGE**
>
> Play twelve-point tiebreakers using the monster formation on every serve.

CHIP LOB RETURN

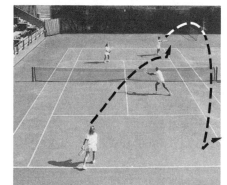

2. *Receiving Team*.
   a. *Chip lob return*. Practice it often, especially against a team that poaches frequently and on second serve returns.

HINT: The receiving team can use the chip lob return as a means to get to the net.

   b. *Playing back*. Both members of the receiving team stay back and work the point.

HINT: Try to keep the ball in play as long as possible, and use high, defensive lobs rather than lower percentage topspin lobs. Each receiver returns four consecutive points. *REMEMBER:* It takes a lot of practice to learn to play back well. However, it can be very effective to neutralize "power" tennis by the serving team.

APPENDIX A Organization of Tennis

ADMINISTRATIVE ORGANIZATION

The United States is divided into seventeen geographic sections, all governed by the United States Tennis Association (USTA). Each section is responsible for promoting and governing tennis in its own area. Groupings in local and national competition are determined by sex and age.

Junior events are those for ages 12, 14, 16, and 18 and under. Youths may enter specific age group competitions each year, provided they do not exceed the maximum age in that age group by the last day of the month during which the tournament is scheduled to start. A bridge between local and national competition for youths is termed "zonal" competition. The United States is divided into four geographic zones for zonal play and offers competition for boys and girls ages 12, 14, and 16 and under.

An adult may play in any age group corresponding to that person's age or less, if he or she reaches the minimum age of that age group anytime prior to December 31. Competition for men and women is held for those over 18, 25, 30, 35, 40, 45, 50, 55, 60, 65, 70, 75, 80, and 85 (men only) in singles, doubles, and often mixed doubles. An "open" age group permits competitors of any age to play.

There are additional doubles events for mother–daughter, father–son, senior mother–daughter and senior father–son. Wheelchair tennis has become increasingly popular as well.

Each of the seventeen geographic sections of the country has almost weekly competition in many age groups during the playing season, which is year-round in some climates. Regular "circuits" of play are established within and between sections, and local and national rankings in each category are published annually. Information regarding competition opportunities can be obtained from each sectional headquarters. All active tennis players should be members of the USTA.

To obtain information about USTA membership, the promotion of tennis as a lifetime sport, teacher training workshops, programs for parks and schools, amateur competition and leagues, recreation and community associations, publications and audiovisual aids, and information regarding facilities, contact:

USTA
70 West Red Oak Lane
White Plains, NY 10604-3602
(914) 696-7000
Fax (914) 696-7167
www.usta.com

For information about national teams, touring pros, top-level junior competition, sports science, and area training centers, contact:
USTA Player Development Office
7310 Crandon Boulevard
Key Biscayne, FL 33149
(305) 365-8782
Fax (305) 365-8700

USTA SECTIONAL ADDRESSES

Caribbean Tennis Association
Box 40456
San Juan, PR 00940-0439
(787) 724-7425
Fax (787) 724-7990

USTA/Eastern, Inc.
550 Mamaroneck Avenue
Suite 505
Harrison, NY 10528
(914) 698-0414
Fax (914) 698-2471

USTA/Florida Section
1280 S.W. 36th Avenue
Suite 305
Pompano Beach, FL 33069-4868
(954) 968-3434
Fax (954) 968-3986

USTA/Hawaii Pacific Section
2615 South King Street
Suite 2A
Honolulu, HI 96826
(808) 955-6696
Fax (808) 955-8363

USTA/Intermountain Section
1201 South Parker Road, #200
Denver, CO 80231
(303) 695-4117
Fax (303) 695-6518

USTA/Mid-Atlantic Section
2230 George C. Marshall Drive
Suite E
Falls Church, VA 22043
(703) 560-9480
Fax (703) 560-9505

USTA/Middle States Section
460 Glennis Circle
King of Prussia, PA 19406
(610) 277-4040
Fax (610) 239-8999

USTA/Midwest Section
8720 Castle Creek Parkway
Suite 329
Indianapolis, IN 46250-4332
(317) 577-5130
Fax (317) 577-5131

USTA/Missouri Valley Section
801 Walnut, Suite 100
Kansas City, MO 64106
(816) 472-6882
Fax (816) 472-6677

USTA/New England
181 Wells Avenue
Newton Centre, MA 02159-3316
(617) 964-2030
Fax (617) 244-8973

USTA/Northern California
1350 S. Loop Road
Suite 100
Alameda, CA 94502-7081
(510) 748-7373
Fax (510) 748-7377

USTA/Northern Section
1001 W. 98th Street
Suite 101
Bloomington, MN 55431
(612) 887-5001
Fax (612) 887-5061

USTA/Pacific Northwest Section
4840 S.W. Western Avenue
Suite 300
Beaverton, OR 97005-3430
(503) 520-1877
Fax (503) 520-0133

USTA/Southern California Section
P.O. Box 240015
Los Angeles, CA 90024-9115
(310) 208-3838
Nighttime/Weekend: (310) 208-3840
Fax (310) 824-7691

USTA/Southern Section
Spalding Woods Office Park
3850 Holcomb Bridge Road
Suite 305
Norcross, GA 30092
(770) 368-8200
Fax (770) 368-9091

USTA/Southwest Section
6240 E. Thomas Road
Suite 302
Scottsdale, AZ 85251
(602) 947-9293
Fax (602) 947-1102

USTA/Texas Station
2111 Dickson
Suite 33
Austin, TX 78704
(512) 443-1334
Fax (512) 443-4748

OTHER MAJOR ORGANIZATIONS

The Association of Tennis Professionals (ATP)
200 ATP Tour Boulevard
Ponte Verde Beach, FL 32082
(904) 285-8000
Fax (904) 285-5966
www.atptour.com

This organization of male tennis-playing professionals is instrumental in the administration of the men's professional tournament circuit and concerns itself with the conduct and welfare of its members. For up-to-date tournament results, tour and ranking information, visit www.atptour.com.

Intercollegiate Tennis Association (ITA)
P.O. Box 71
Princeton, NJ 08544
(609) 258-6332
Fax (609) 258-2935

This organization of men's and women's college and community college coaches promotes the collegiate game and the coaches' profession.

International Tennis Federation (ITF)
Palliser Road, Barons Court
London W14 9EN, England
011-44-71-381-8060
Fax 011-44-171-381-5965
www.itftennis.com

This is the governing body of international tennis, and it establishes the rules of tennis. The USTA is a member of this organization.

International Tennis Hall of Fame
Newport Casino
194 Bellevue Avenue
Newport, RI 02840
(401) 849-3990
Fax (401) 849-8780
www.tennisfame.org

This is a nonprofit agency dedicated to preserving the history of tennis worldwide.

National Collegiate Athletic Association (NCAA)
6201 College Boulevard
Overland Park, KS 66211
(913) 339-1906
Fax (913) 339-0032
www.ncaa.org

This organization governs intercollegiate athletics. The relevance to tennis is that many of its rules apply to definitions of amateurism and recruiting of high school tennis players.

U.S. Professional Tennis Association (USPTA)
One USPTA Centre
3535 Briarpark Drive
Houston, TX 77042
(713) 978-7782
Fax (713) 978-7780
e-mail: uspta@uspta.org
www.uspta.org

This organization of certified U.S. teaching professionals promotes the profession of teaching tennis and administers an extensive professional teacher certification program.

U.S. Professional Tennis Registry (USPTR)
P.O. Box 4739
Hilton Head Island, SC 29938
(843) 785-7244
Fax (843) 686-2033
www.usptr.org/hmpg.htm

This organization also certifies teaching professionals and has an extensive training program for those wishing to become professional tennis teachers.

Women's Tennis Association (WTA)
133 First Street N.E.
St. Petersburg, FL 33701
(813) 895-5000
Fax (813) 894-1982
www.corelwtatour.com

This organization of female tennis-playing professionals is responsible for the women's professional circuit and promotes the tennis welfare of its members.

Tennis Industry Association
200 Castlewood Drive
N. Palm Beach, FL 33408-5666
(407) 848-1026
Fax (407) 863-8984

This organization represents the collaboration of organizations involved in the tennis industry—sporting goods manufacturers, equipment manufacturers, etc.—who have bonded together to promote the game of tennis.

U.S. Tennis Court & Track Builders Association
3525 Ellicott Mills Drive, Suite N
Ellicott City, MD 21043
(410) 418-4875
Fax (410) 418-4805

This organization provides information on tennis court construction.

TENNIS PUBLICATIONS

The USTA is a tremendous resource for the teacher of tennis. The annual pamphlet "Tennis Publication" lists by subject most current tennis book-type publications. The listing includes a descriptive paragraph about each publication and video, the cost, and how to obtain the materials.

College Tennis Weekly
P.O. Box 24379
Edina, MN 55424
(612) 920-8947
Fax (612) 920-8940
www.tennisnews.com

Focus is on collegiate match and tournament results, player and team rankings, and general college tennis news.

Notes and Netcords
1266 E. Main Street, 4th Floor
Stamford, CT 06902
(203) 978-1740
Fax (203) 978-1702

This is the official weekly publication of the Women's Tennis Association. It includes professional tournament schedules, results, and the latest computerized rankings.

Tennis Direct
1463 Premier Road
Troy, MI 48084
(800) 247-8273
Fax (248) 637-8832

Tennis Magazine
810 Seventh Avenue, 4th Floor
New York, NY 10019
(212) 636-2764
Fax (212) 636-2730
To subscribe: (800) 666-8336

This monthly periodical is the official magazine of the USTA and includes a supplement called "Tennis, USTA," which contains specific news from all seventeen USTA sections. In addition to editorials, human interest stories, tournament reports, and instructional articles, special annual features include (1) a review on rackets and other equipment, and (2) a listing of all tennis camps.

www.tennisdirect.com
A mail-order catalog company specializing in all things related to tennis. A great source for books and videos.

Tennis Week
341 Madison Avenue
Suite 600
New York, NY 10017
(212) 808-4750
Fax (212) 983-6302
www.tennisweek.com

This tennis weekly provides up-to-date rankings of the international men's and women's pro tours, as well as extensive listings of professional tour results of all levels of ATP and WTA events. Its articles appeal to the general tennis enthusiast.

USTA College Tennis Guide
% USTA
70 West Red Oak Lane
White Plains, NY 10604-3602
(914) 696-7000
Fax (914) 696-7167

This publication is a must for the prospective college tennis player. Information about more than 1,300 U.S. universities, colleges, and junior colleges is presented. The coach, address, size of school, level of competition, scholarship information, and much more is provided.

USTA Yearbook
152 The Lynnway
Lynn, MA 01902
(781) 598-9230
Fax (781) 599-4018

The yearbook contains complete tennis rules, USTA age-group rankings, championship results, sectional information and member club address lists, and historical results of the world's top events. Published by H. O. Zimman, Inc.

COMPETITIONS

Until 1968, tournaments of any consequence were open only to amateurs (players ineligible to receive prize money). A limited number of professionals (usually the best one or two amateurs each year "turned pro" in order to play for money) played mostly barnstorming exhibition matches throughout the world. Tournaments, in order to secure the best players, paid so much "under the table" to attract the top amateurs that many amateurs were actually making more money than the pros. In an effort to end this hypocrisy, the British, in 1968, opened Wimbledon—the most important tournament in the world—to amateurs and professionals alike, and also offered prize money. Since then, all major international tournaments have been opened to professionals as well as amateurs (mostly college students and younger, who are ineligible for prize money).

Another significant development is the increasing number of major tournaments played indoors, especially in winter months, in the United States and Europe, making tennis a year-round sport for spectators as well as players.

Major World Team Competitions

Davis Cup (established in 1900). Almost 100 countries send their top male players to this competition. The top 16 teams participate in a single elimination tournament—the *World Group*—for the championship, while the remaining countries play in three *zonal* groupings: the American, the Euro/African, and the Asia/Oceania.

The zonal groupings are subdivided into Groups I, II, III, and IV. The countries move up or down a group depending on the previous year's results. Each round of play consists of a three-day match: two singles on the first day, one doubles match on the second day, and two singles on the third day.

The Fed Cup (established in 1963). The International Lawn Tennis Federation initiated this international team competition for women. The format for competition is modeled closely on the Davis Cup for men, with a world group and levels of zonal qualifying groupings. Play consists of two singles on the first day, one doubles on the second day, and two singles on the third day.

The Olympic Games. Tennis was included in the Olympics from 1896 until 1924. It reappeared as a full official sport in the 1988 Olympic Games.

Age-Group Competitions. There are several established international age-group team competitions for seniors.

Major Individual Competitions

The top international tournaments (now all "open" events) are the All-England Championships (Wimbledon), the United States Championships (Flushing Meadows, New York), the French Championships, and the Australian Championships. Play consists of single elimination-type competition. Only six players have ever completed a "grand slam" by winning all four tournaments in succession: Don Budge, Maureen Connolly, and Martina Navratilova of the United States, Rod Laver (twice) and Margaret Smith Court of Australia, and Steffi Graf of Germany.

The Grand Slam Cup, established in 1990, is a year-end indoor competition composed of male professionals who have recorded the best performance at the four Grand Slam Tournaments during the year. The Grand Slam Cup is held in Europe and is indicative of the European Community's growing influence on the world's men's tennis circuit, especially in fall and winter indoor events.

Professionally, both men and women now compete in year-round Grand Prix "circuits" during which they accumulate points that can lead to bonus prize money at the end of the year. Play is indoors and out, and on all types of surfaces. There are several tiers of competition, which are determined largely by the amount of prize money offered. These range from Future and Satellite circuits up to Challenger events, each with qualifying tournaments that give lesser players a chance to work their way up to the major events. Computer points based on weekly results are awarded and form the basis for rankings, which, for the most part, determine tournament eligibility.

Also there are circuits and tournaments for every age group in the United States. The "older" junior events, in addition to sectional play, feature a "national circuit" in the summer months. National junior championships include a "feed-in" consolation event up through the quarterfinals.

Other Competitions

Beginning tennis players are often faced with the problem of finding practice partners and opponents of comparable ability. Many city recreation departments oversee public tennis clubs for adults that offer various levels of competition for a nominal annual fee. Many areas have tennis patron organizations to promote all levels of competition for youths.

League Tennis. The USTA League program offers team competition for men, women, and youths. Teams begin play at the local level and can progress to district and/or sectional levels, and finally to the national team championships. For men and women, League play is conducted at the 2.5, 3.0, 3.5, 4.0, 4.5, and 5.0 ability level. For senior men and women (over age 50) play is at 3.0, 3.5, 4.0, and 4.5 levels on the National Tennis Rating System scale. Call your USTA section to find the date and location of "Verification of Rating" clinics nearest you. Ask for the name of the local league coordinator who helps to assign interested parties to teams.

Grand Slam Websites

Australian Open: www.ausopen.org
French Open: www.frenchopen.org
U.S. Open: www.usopen.org
Wimbledon: www.wimbledon.org

THE NATIONAL TENNIS RATING SYSTEM

The USTA, the USPTA, and the International Racquet Sports Association have developed a self-rating system to help individuals determine their relative level of play for school, club, and community programs as well as for leagues and tournaments. (To "rate" yourself, assume you are playing someone of the same sex and ability, and be certain you qualify on all points of all preceding categories, as well as those in the classification you choose.) The "General Characteristics of Various Playing Levels" of the National Tennis Rating System are as follows:

1.0 This player is just starting to play tennis.

1.5 This player has limited experience and is still working primarily on getting the ball into play.

2.0 This player needs on-court experience. This player has obvious stroke weaknesses but is familiar with basic positions for singles and doubles play.

2.5 This player is learning to judge where the ball is going, although court coverage is weak. This player can sustain a rally of slow pace with other players of the same ability.

3.0 This player is consistent when hitting medium-paced shots, but is not comfortable with all strokes and lacks control when trying for directional intent, depth, or power.

3.5 This player has achieved improved stroke dependability and direction on moderate shots, but still lacks depth and variety. This player is starting to exhibit more aggressive net play, has improved court coverage, and is developing teamwork in doubles.

4.0 This player has dependable strokes, including directional intent and depth on both forehand and backhand sides on moderate shots, plus the ability to use lobs, overheads, approach shots, and volleys with some success. This player occasionally forces errors when serving, and teamwork in doubles is evident.

4.5 This player has begun to master the use of power and spins and is beginning to handle pace, has sound footwork, can control depth of shots, and is beginning to vary tactics according to opponents. This player can hit first serves with power and accuracy and place the second serve and is able to rush net successfully.

5.0 This player has good shot anticipation and frequently has an outstanding shot or exceptional consistency around which a game may be structured. This player can regularly hit winners or force errors off of short balls and can put away volleys, can successfully execute lobs, drop shots, half volleys, and overhead smashes, and has good depth and spin on most second serves.

5.5 This player has developed power and/or consistency as a major weapon. This player can vary strategies and styles of play in a competitive situation and hits dependable shots in a stress situation.

6.0
to
7.0 These players will generally not need NTRP ratings. Rankings or past rankings will speak for themselves. The 6.0 player typically has had intensive training for national tournament competition at the junior level and collegiate levels and has obtained a sectional and/or national ranking. The 6.5 player has a reasonable chance of succeeding at the 7.0 level and has extensive satellite tournament experience. The 7.0 is a world class player who is committed to tournament competition on the international level and whose major source of income is tournament prize winnings.

For the Teacher

PRESENTING THE BASICS OF TENNIS

Use Chapter 2 as your guide.

Private Lessons. The instructor simply replaces the tosser in the photographs and uses the verbal cues (***bold italics***) as a guide for the pupil. The progressions and court positions remain the same. Be certain the concepts of the Basic Strokes and accompanying **corrections** are understood before moving onto the Ball Machine for additional practice.

Class or Group Lessons. The learning method as presented in Part 1 of this book is simple and extremely effective as a teaching method, if followed exactly. This is especially true of the verbal cues, which can be thought of as "instructor commands," as well as of the learning progressions of the Basic Strokes in Chapter 2 and Basic Strategy in Chapters 4 and 5. The instructor initially literally leads the class through each hit of the ball using these **verbal cues** ("commands").

To help the instructor adapt the **court positions** to a class, multiples of six are used for each court or each side of the net. The T's on the court help define areas from which to hit, and light chalk marks can help to designate where the balls should be tossed for groundstroke practice. (Chalk can help define hitting positions for serving, etc., as well.) These court positions are used for practice of the Basic Strokes.

BASIC COURT POSITIONS FOR CLASS LEARNING GROUNDSTROKES

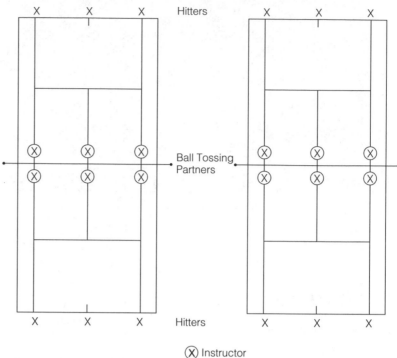

Ⓧ Instructor

UNIT PLAN— BEGINNING TENNIS

Lesson I
  Discuss—History
  Forehand & Backhand
    (Stationary/Adjusting)

Lesson II
  Discuss—Equipment
  Forehand & Backhand:
    Adjusting
    Running

Lesson III
  Discuss—Courts
  Forehand & Backhand:
    Running Wide
    Short & Deep

Lesson IV
  Backhand—Running Wide
  Forehand—Alley Rally:
    One-Hit

Lesson V
  Serve
  Backhand—Running Wide
  Forehand—Alley Rally:
    Two-Hit

Lesson VI
  Serve
  Backhand—Running Wide
  Forehand—Alley Rally:
    Two-Hit
    Forever Rally

Lesson VII
  Serve
  Crosscourt Rally:
    Two-Hit
    Forever Rally (Gradually
      Move to Full Court)

Lesson VIII
  Serve & Return
  Crosscourt Rally:
    Two-Hit (Full Court)
    Forever (Full Court)

Lesson IX
  Discuss—Etiquette
  Serve & Return
  Volley—Forehand & Backhand
  Overhead

Lesson X
  Discuss—Rules & Scoring
  Singles—Play Games

Lesson XI
  Discuss—Doubles Positions
    & Responsibilities
  Doubles—Situations:
    Crosscourt Rally

Lesson XII
  Doubles Situations:
    Crosscourt Rally Review
    Lobs—Short & Deep

Lesson XIII
  Doubles—Situations:
    Review
    Random Points

Lesson XIV
  Review—Doubles Positions
    & Responsibilities
  Random Points
  Discuss—Server & Receiver
  Play Points Using Serve

Lesson XV
  Doubles—Play games

Lesson XVI
  Begin Doubles Tournament

"TOURNAMENT" PLAY

For intermediate- and advanced-level classes, instruction in smaller groups, perhaps even with the use of ball-throwing machines, can be mixed with "tournament" play. Here follow descriptions of four types of tournaments that could be conducted within class time or on the pupils' own time: (1) Ladder Tournament, (2) Round Robin, (3) Single Elimination Tournament with Feed-in Consolation, and (4) Compass Tournament.

Ladder Tournament. In a ladder tournament, the players are ranked according to their ability from top to bottom in a vertical line. The tournament is a continuous affair, and a player can "challenge" anyone no more than three places ahead of him or her on the ladder. If player E challenges player C and wins, player E assumes the number 3 position, player C assumes the number 4 position, and player D is automatically moved down into the number 5 position. If player E challenges player C and loses, ladder positions remain unchanged.

A ladder tournament is largely self-sustaining, provided a clear set of rules is posted. These rules should pertain to the amount of time a player has to accept a challenge, how soon a rematch may be scheduled, and so on.

1. _____A_____
2. _____B_____
3. _____C_____
4. _____D_____
5. _____E_____
6. _____F_____
7. _____G_____
8. _____H_____

Round-Robin. In a round-robin tournament, everyone plays everyone else. Because a round-robin is difficult to finish if there are too many players, a tournament director might consider a series of four-player round-robins and then have all the winners play in an additional round-robin, the second-place finishers do the same, and so on.

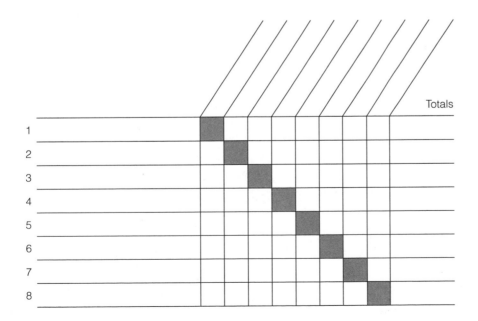

Single Elimination Tournament. A draw is "seeded" so that hypothetically the two best players would not meet until the finals, the top four until the semifinals, and the top eight until the quarterfinals. If there is not a full draw, "Byes" may be given, generally to the highest seeded players.

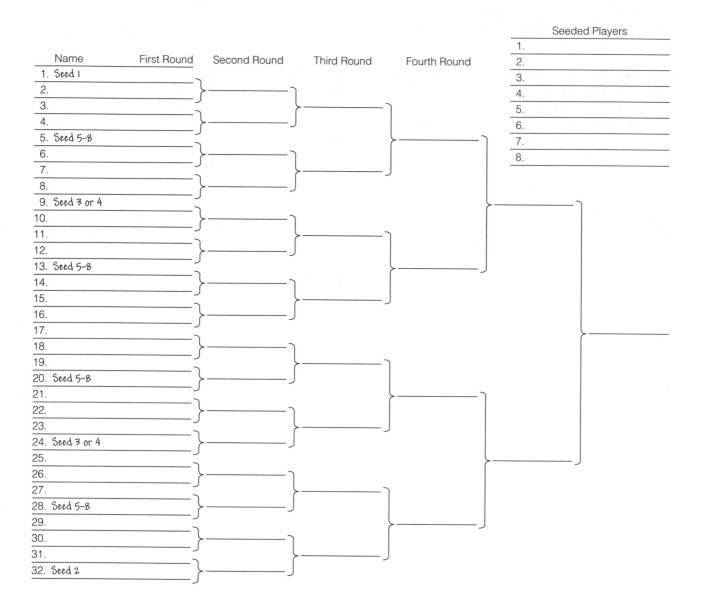

Feed-in Consolation. To give most everyone a "second chance," a supplemental feed-in draw is included for a single elimination tournament.

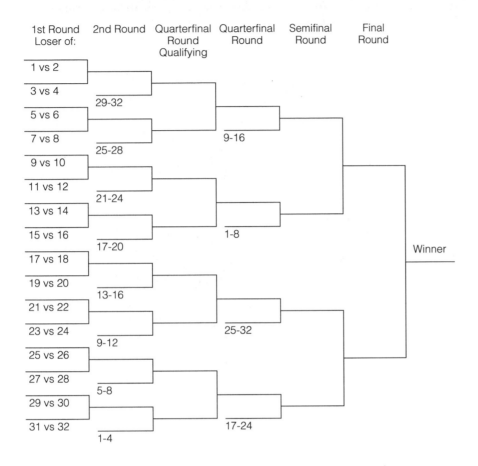

Compass Tournament. A tournament adopted by the USTA that guarantees multiple matches (16 players = 4 matches each). Players move in compass directions (East—to the right; North—up; etc.) depending upon whether they win or lose. This determines their next opponent.

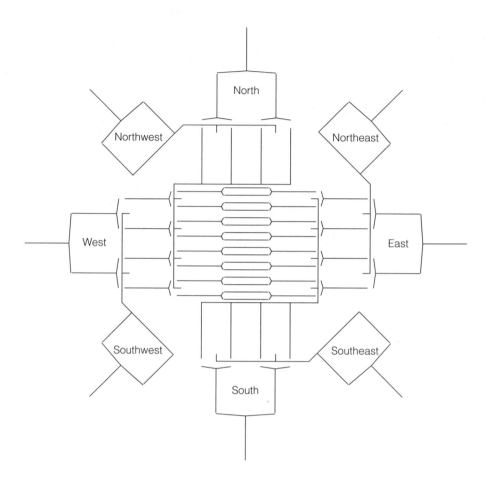

For the Coach

ORGANIZING A MEANINGFUL PRACTICE WORKOUT

The total time spent on workouts and the method of practicing will vary depending upon individual needs and differences, the nearness of competition dates, and other factors. However, as a general rule, most individuals will improve rapidly and probably near the maximum pace with a formal five-day workout plan. Including prepractice warm-up and post-practice conditioning, the total time spent would amount to about 3–3½ hours per day. However, on court, tennis time is about 2–2½ hours. One day a week should be completely away from tennis, and the sixth day should be an optional workout day—either no play, light hitting, or perhaps a singles or doubles match.

On the five formal practice days, about one-third of the practice time will include a General Warm-up (15 minutes of light jogging or footwork drills, followed by stretching), and a Conditioning Program (approximately 30 minutes at the conclusion of practice, alternating between Strength Training and Intensive Running). The start of each practice should be allotted to a discussion of the goals of the day's workout.

Of the remaining hitting/practice time, one-half should be devoted to Basic Groove Hitting and Partner Rallies. This includes work on serve and serve return, groundstrokes, net play, and net approach and defense. The second half is devoted to Practice of Game Situations and Playing, including both singles and doubles. The skill emphasis and time allotment will vary depending upon individual needs and the weekly or seasonal competition schedule.

The chart on the facing page illustrates how a weekly schedule can be organized. Note the variety of ways that each of the above areas of **Warm-up and Conditioning, Basic Groove Hitting and Partner Rallies,** and **Game Situations and Playing** are addressed.

In addition, here's a Sample Warm-up Session that's an especially good workout to use as a prelude to intrasquad set play:

A Sample Warm-up Session (approximately one hour)

Jog, jump ropes, stretch

Backcourt (Both players back)
   General Groundstroke Hit
   Slice Backhand Rally
   Crosscourt; Down-Line Rally

Net Play (One player at net; the other, back)
   Forehand Volleys
   Backhand Volleys
   Backcourt—Hit Down Line; Net—Volley Crosscourt
   Lob/Overhead Warm-up
   Up (Overheads); Back (Lobs)

Serve (Cones as targets)
   Serve to Center T's (Warm-ups)
   Serve—Wide; Return

Sample Weekly Workout Schedule

Time	Drill	Monday	Tuesday	Wednesday	Thursday	Friday
2:00	Warm-up Meeting	Jump rope Stretch	Jog/footwork mix Stretch	Jump rope Stretch	Jog/footwork mix Stretch	Follow-the-leader Stretch
2:30	Serve Return	**Serve** Wide **Return** Cut the angle	**Serve** Center **T** **Return** To a spot	**Serve** Deuce court: wide; center **T** **Return** Stand in and drive	**Serve** Ad court: wide; center **T** **Return** To a spot	**Serve** Deuce and Ad court: wide; center **T** **Return** Stand in and chip
2:45	Basic groove hitting and partner rallies	Ball machine circuit: 1. Oscillation groundstrokes 2. Oscillation low volleys 3. Overheads 4. 3-shot approach drill	1. Serve and volley (2 on 1) 2. Passing shot drill 3. Doubles points (1 up; 1 back)	1. Crosscourt/Down the line a. Both back b. 1 up; 1 back 2. 2 on 1 (2 up; 1 back) 3. Volley rally a. Quick volleys b. Single-file approach	1. Serve and volley (4-hit drill) 2. Up and back 3. Doubles points (both close)	1. Crosscourt rally; approach down line on first short ball 2. Cross-court points (1 up; 1 back) 3. Serve and volley scramble
3:45	Game situations and playing	1. Serve and volley points a. Bumper tennis. **Emphasize** Server: 2-shot combinations Receiver: To a spot 2. Doubles Servers: Signals (poach often) Receivers: Both back and work point	1. Backcourt points a. Rotate: 2 more errors than placements (**Emphasize** Patience) 2. Serve: 4 games or until broken (**Emphasize** Serve and volley on most first serves) Receiver: Try different plan each game	1. Serve and volley points to 7. **Emphasize** Server: 2-shot combinations Receiver: First serve—use lob on second shot; second serve—attack or run around 2. Doubles a. Servers: On first serve monster or Aussie b. Receivers: Close (some chip lobs)	1. Backcourt points a. Bumper tennis. **Emphasize** Attack on short ball 2. Singles: 5-5, finish set (include tiebreaker)	1. Singles sets
4:45	Conditioning	Strength training	Conditioning	Strength training	Conditioning	Strength training

APPENDIX D Physical Conditioning for the Tennis Player

A physical conditioning program should accomplish two goals: Your ability to perform maximally over time should increase, and the chance of injury should be greatly minimized. The well-conditioned body can handle maximum physical exertion with minimal effort.

Cardiorespiratory efficiency, the ability to perform reasonable physical activity over an extended period of time, is an indicator of your physical condition. It is measured largely by how efficiently the heart and lungs supply the body's increased need for oxygen during moderate but sustained physical activity known as *aerobic exercise*. The obvious result is that you become less winded during physical exercise. Examples are jogging, fast walking, aerobic dancing, and swimming.

Measuring the Extent of Your Exercise. In order to improve your cardiorespiratory efficiency, the goal of your exercise should be to increase your heart rate to approximately 70–85 percent of your "maximum" heart rate. The increased heart rate should be reached and sustained for 15–20 minutes three to five times per week, and should result in good, general aerobic physical condition.

An easy way to calculate your maximum heart rate is to subtract your age from 220. For example, if you are 20 years old, your exercise heart rate should increase to 70–85 percent of 200, or 140–170 beats per minute.

Increase in physical efficiency delays fatigue and hastens recovery. Fatigue hinders maximum performance and makes injury more likely. If any injury persists after using ice, elevation, and rest, see your doctor for professional advice.

PRE-PRACTICE WARM-UP

The workout warm-up is intended to get the body ready for exercise and may take up to 15 minutes to complete. A light jog several times around the court mixing in slides, crossovers, back pedals, skips, and big arm movements, followed by a few moments of rapid rope-jumping, serves to increase the heartbeat and blood flow. Follow with a stretch of the main muscle groups (examples are depicted on page 114) to limber up the muscles and to help prevent muscle tears and pulls.

HINTS: **NOURISHMENT**

Drink: Fluid replacement is a key factor in avoiding cramps, especially during warm and hot days. When playing in an environment where heat and humidity encourage dehydration, begin drinking extra fluids at least two to three days in advance of competition. During competition, drink 4–8 ounces of fluid every changeover (approximately every 5–10 minutes). Plain water is fine, but if you wish to use a flavored sports drink fortified with electrolytes, dilute the product by mixing at least two parts of water for every part of sports drink. Remember, if you wait until you first "feel" thirsty, it is too late to adequately replace fluids.

Food: A balanced diet incorporating the basic food groups of carbohydrates, fats, and proteins is essential for good health. However, here are some extra tips for the athlete. Bananas and oranges are good on-court sources of extra potassium, which can also be a deterrent to cramping. Intensive activity causes the athlete to rapidly deplete glycogen, the main form of stored carbohydrates, which is used to provide energy to the muscles. Therefore, prematch meals should be rich in carbohydrates. Examples are: pancakes, baked potatoes, pasta, breads, and starchy vegetables. Studies have shown that an immediate (15–30 minutes) post-competition snack, such as bagels, replaces glycogen stores more quickly and efficiently. Sports bars can be helpful as well, in terms of replenishing some of the body's basic nutrition needs.

SAMPLE STRETCHES

1. Shoulders (Deltoid muscles) (Arms over head)

2. Shoulders (Deltoid muscles) (Arms behind back)

3. Trunk (Abdominals and latissimus dorsi)

4. Thigh (Quadriceps)

5. Calf (Gastrocnemius)

6. Groin

7. Hamstrings

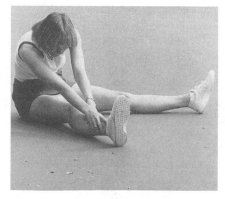

Of course, when actually beginning to hit balls, a player should emphasize smooth and fluid motions and only gradually accelerate the speed of body movement and the hit itself. Sometimes beginning the warm-up rally in the service squares and gradually moving back to full court helps to emphasize this. *IMPORTANT*: Substantial stretching should also be incorporated into every *post*-workout routine, whether it be simply doing tennis or conditioning.

CURL-UPS

PUSH-UPS

PRESEASON CONDITIONING PROGRAM

An Interval Training Program

Tennis is primarily an anaerobic activity. That is, since tennis demands relatively short, explosive bursts of energy (as opposed to the more sustained energy use of distance swimming and jogging), the tennis player's body must be trained to withstand fatigue for short activity periods with decreased oxygen supply.

An efficient method of conditioning for anaerobic activity is *interval training*, which consists of high-intensity running over prescribed distances with prescribed rest periods. Running is done for distances of 110, 220, and 440 yards.

The 110- and 220-yard runs require a period of relief (in other words, active rest, such as a fast walk or easy jog) about three times the duration of the run. The 440-yard run requires a relief time of about twice the duration of the run. (Complete inactivity between running bouts will result only in early fatigue.)

Interval training can take place every other day (a day's rest is needed for the body to recover) or twice a week, but the total distance run is increased each week. You should time yourself with a stopwatch each day. (Caution: If you are not in reasonable condition when you begin interval training, you may wish to start with a reduced schedule totaling from one-half to three-quarters of a mile.) A poorly conditioned player should complete at least several days of aerobic fitness exercises to help reduce body stress before beginning an initial interval-training program. Remember to always have a "cool-down" period at the end—some light jogging or walking and always some stretching. (Once a certain condition level is reached, 95 percent of it can be retained with one workout a week.)

Adjacent is a sample eight-week schedule that builds from one mile to a total distance of two miles per workout.

Week 1 (1 mile; 1760 yards)
Tuesday: 2 × 440; 2 × 220; 4 × 110
Thursday: 2 × 440; 4 × 220

Week 2 (1⅛ miles; 1980 yards)
Tuesday: 2 × 440; 3 × 220; 4 × 110
Thursday: 2 × 440; 5 × 220

Week 3 (1¼ miles; 2200 yards)
Tuesday: 2 × 440; 4 × 220; 4 × 110
Thursday: 2 × 440; 6 × 220

Week 4 (1⅜ miles; 2420 yards)
Tuesday: 2 × 440; 4 × 220; 6 × 110
Thursday: 2 × 440; 7 × 220

Week 5 (1½ miles; 2640 yards)
Tuesday: 2 × 440; 4 × 220; 8 × 110
Thursday: 2 × 440; 8 × 220

Week 6 (1⅝ miles; 2860 yards)
Tuesday: 3 × 440; 3 × 220; 8 × 110
Thursday: 3 × 440; 7 × 220

Week 7 (1¾ miles; 3080 yards)
Tuesday: 3 × 440; 4 × 220; 8 × 110
Thursday: 3 × 440; 8 × 220

Week 8 (2 miles; 3520 yards)
Tuesday: 4 × 440; 4 × 220; 8 × 110
Thursday: 4 × 440; 8 × 220

IN-SEASON CONDITIONING

Agility and Running Drills

In-season conditioning should feature shorter bursts of speed and power as well as reaction and agility routines. You should vary the workouts described in this section in order to keep players fresh and interested.

Fartleks. (Recommendation: Use a soft surface such as grass.) This workout features a continuous jog, mixed with short bursts of various footwork drills and sprints over an expanding and variable linear course for 20 to 25 minutes nonstop. Use markers (two cones, for example) to establish the length of the course, which will range from 20 to 35 yards. *Example:* (1) Begin by jogging from one cone 20 yards to around the second cone for 3–4 minutes as a warm-up. (2) Continue to always jog back to the second cone, but add various mixes when going out from the original starting cone: sprints, slides, crossovers, butt whacks, thigh slaps, giant skips, back pedals, hops (one foot, both feet), lunges, etc. (3) Alternate sprints with other exercises on each trip out, but always return by jogging back. (4) Increase the number and length of the sprints in the middle of the workout. (5) As the workout draws to a close, "shorten the course." (6) Finish with 3–4 minutes of light jogging followed by a good stretch.

HINT: The coach can serve as the starting cone and can expand or shorten the course by moving farther away from or closer to the second cone. The coach also can dictate what the specific mix will be as the players go by.

HINT: A source for ladders, cones, medicine balls, hurdles, etc., is Power Systems, Inc., 2933 Northwest Park Drive, P.O. Box 12620, Knoxville, TN 37912. Phone (800) 321-6975 or (423) 947-5229; Fax (800) 298-2057 or (423) 947-0319.

Follow-the-Leader. The coach and the team face each other from a distance of about 10 yards. The team begins by running lightly and quickly in place. The coach uses commands to tell the team how and when to move in explosive bursts: "Jog" (run in place); "Slide" or "Crossover" (coach points in the direction the team should move, changing direction often); "Forward" and "Set-React" (using a split stop, followed by an imitation of a low volley); "Back" (using crossover steps with racket arm up, emulating preparation for an overhead); and "Hit" (the players use a scissor kick as if hitting an overhead and then recover by running forward). Use several combinations of commands, and work continuously for 1–2 minutes. Then rest and repeat.

Ball Drills. The team divides into pairs, and partners face each other about eight feet apart. Partner 1 has two tennis balls and is kneeling; Partner 2 is in a crouch ready to move. *Basic Drill:* Partner 1 rolls the ball forward to either side of partner 2. Partner 2 slides to the ball, bends from the knees (not back) to pick it up and returns it by bouncing it back to partner 1 and recovers by sliding back to the starting point. Partner 1 rolls the second ball to the other side, and the drill repeats. After 60–90 seconds, the partners switch positions. *Step 2:* Repeat Basic Drill, but partner 1 adds the command "Check" after partner 2 returns the ball. On this command, partner 2 sprints forward and touches the outstretched hand of partner 1, then returns by backpeddling to the original position and resumes sliding. Switch positions and repeat. *Step 3:* Repeat Basic Drill, but partner 1 adds command "Back." On this command, partner 2 quickly turns and runs back approximately 8 feet and touches the court with one hand (position partners so that a court line can be used as a reference to touch). Return to starting position and resume slides. Switch positions and repeat. *Step 4:* Repeat Basic Drill, but partner 1 adds command "Circle." Partner 2 sprints forward and runs around partner 1, and then backpedals to starting position and resumes sliding. Switch positions and repeat. *Step 5:* Repeat Basic Drill, but randomly mix commands of "Check," "Back," and "Circle." Switch partners.

Obstacle Course. The coach establishes eight to ten various stations on a "course" spread out over two to four courts. Players follow one another every 15 seconds through the course. Stations might include: (1) rope ladders (or chalked ladders) laid on the court for hops, short steps, or steps to the side in and out of the ladder; (2) hurdles (or cones) of different sizes to hop over; (3) crunches; (4) push-ups; (5) cones to zigzag around; (6) medicine balls; (7) "rubber bands" attached to a fence post for resistance work.

Harness Training. (Work in pairs.) Partner 1 holds the ends of harness band that is around the waist of partner 2. *Basic Drill:* Partner 2 sprints forward for 10–15 yards, pulling partner 1, who offers proper resistance to "challenge" partner 2. Repeat several times, then switch partners. *Variations:* (1) Sprint out at different angles from partner 1; (2) incorporate split stop and reach for low volley; (3) jump out from one foot to the other, with partner 1 off to the side; and (4) incorporate backpedals.

A Weight-Training Program

Weight training consists of a series of progressive resistance exercises for specific muscle groups of the body. (For more information see *Basic Weight Training* by Thomas Fahey, 2000, Mayfield Publishing Company.) Muscle strength (leading to more explosive power and speed) and muscle endurance (enabling the muscles to stay contracted for an extended period of time), as well as increased flexibility, are enhanced by a good weight-training program.

Generally, muscle strength is built best by heavy resistance exercises allowing for only 6–8 repetitions. If the emphasis is to be on muscle endurance, emphasize light resistance, which allows for 15–20 repetitions.

A good general workout for a tennis player can be accomplished in 30 minutes. There should be at least 48 hours, but no more than 96 hours, between workouts. (Once a certain strength level is reached, 95 percent can be retained with one workout a week.)

Never hold your breath while lifting, because the amount of oxygen you receive will be limited and may cause dizziness. Instead, exhale while exerting the greatest force and inhale while returning the weight to the original position.

The workout outlined below is a simple one and affords a compromise in developing both muscle strength and muscle endurance. A particular exercise should be repeated at least 8, and up to 12, times. Each repetition is referred to as a rep. If you cannot do 8 reps, the weight is too heavy. If you can do more than 12 reps, the weight is too light. In the off-season, you will probably use heavier resistance with less repetitions. During the season, you should move to lighter resistance and more repetitions, especially on days prior to matches.

The rate for performing each rep should be about 2 seconds up, about 4 seconds down. Use a full range of motion. If a rep takes 5–6 seconds to complete, the entire exercise set will last about a minute. No more than a minute of rest should be taken before moving on to the next exercise. To help you monitor your improvement, you should keep a record of the weight used and the number of reps achieved for each exercise.

The following exercises are selected especially for tennis players. There are several kinds of weight equipment available. For the sake of simplicity, most of the following exercises are performed on the Nautilus machines. The type of machine, order of exercise, and muscle groups affected are listed. In lieu of weight machines, you can use free weights or elastic bands to replicate exercises for the muscle groups listed.

HINT: Strengthening the abdominal muscles is crucial. Therefore, curl-ups (crunches) should be a part of every strength workout: (1) Lie on your back with your hands clasped behind your head. (2) Your feet should be flat on the ground and your knees bent. (3) Raise your shoulders off the ground, keeping your elbows out to the side and keeping your lower back prone against the ground. (4) Return smoothly to your starting position and repeat. (5) *Variation:* Twist to one side when you raise your shoulders off the ground.

Machine	Order of Exercise	Muscle Groups
a. Hydra Gym	1. Hip abduction/adduction	Groin
b. Nautilus Leg Extension	2. Leg extension	Quadriceps
c. Nautilus Leg Curl	3. Leg curl	Hamstrings
d. Nautilus Double Shoulder	4. Side lateral raise	Deltoids
	5. Seated press	Deltoids (triceps)
e. Nautilus Double Chest	6. Bent arm fly	Pectorals
	7. Decline press	Pectorals (deltoids, triceps)
f. Nautilus Pullover	8. Pullover	Latissimus dorsi
	9. Lateral pulldown	Latissimus dorsi (biceps)
g. Nautilus Bicep-Tricep	10. Biceps curl	Biceps
	11. Triceps extension	Triceps
h. Universal Curl	12. Wrist curls	Wrist flexors (forearms)
	13. Wrist reverse curls	Wrist extensors (forearms)

GLOSSARY

Ace A ball served so well that the opponent has no chance to touch or return it.

Ad Short for "advantage," it is the first point scored after deuce. If the serving side scores, it is "ad in"; if the receiving side scores, it is "ad out."

Ad court The left-hand service court, so called because an "ad" score is served there.

All An even score: 30-all, 3-all, etc.

Alley The area on either side of the singles court that enlarges the width of the court for doubles. Each alley is 4½ feet wide.

American twist A spin serve that causes the ball to bounce high and in the opposite direction from which it was originally traveling.

Angle shot A ball hit to an extreme angle across the court.

Approach A shot behind which a player comes to the net.

Attack drive An aggressive approach shot.

Australian doubles Doubles in which the point begins with the server and server's partner on the same right or left side of the court.

Backcourt The area between the service line and the baseline.

Backhand The stroke used to return balls hit to the left of a right-handed player or to the right of a left-handed player.

Backhand court For a right-handed player, the left-hand side of the court; for a left-handed player, the right-hand side of the court.

Backspin The ball spins from bottom to top (counterclockwise), applied by hitting down and through the ball. Also called "underspin." *See also* Slice, Chop.

Backswing The initial part of any swing. The act of bringing the racket back to the ready-to-hit position to prepare for the forward swing.

Ball person During competition, a person who retrieves balls for the players.

Baseline The end boundary line of a tennis court, located 39 feet from the net.

Bevel The tilt or slant of the racket face.

Boron An expensive, extremely durable material used to manufacture racket frames.

Break service To win a game in which the opponent serves.

Bye In competition, the situation in which a player is not required to play in a particular round.

Cannonball A hard, flat serve.

Center mark The short line that bisects the center of the baseline.

Center service line The line that is perpendicular to the net and divides the two service courts.

Center strap A strap in the center of the net, anchored to the ground to hold the net secure at a height of 3 feet.

Chip A modified slice, used primarily in doubles to return a serve. A chip requires a short swing, which allows the receiver to move in close to return.

Choke up To grip the racket up higher on the handle.

Chop A backspin shot in which the racket moves down through the ball at an angle greater than 45 degrees.

Circuit A series of tournaments.

Closed face The angle of the hitting face of the racket when it is turned down toward the court.

The Code A supplement to the rules of tennis that specifically defines etiquette parameters such as "gamesmanship" and line call responsibilities.

Compass Tournament A tournament that moves players in compass directions of the draw sheet depending on the result of each match.

Composite A racket frame made with two or more materials.

Consolation A tournament in which losers continue to play in a losers' tournament.

Continental grip A grip between the Eastern forehand and backhand that is used for the spin serve and by many players for the forehand and backhand volley.

Conventional Refers to racquet heads that are less than 90 square inches.

Crosscourt shot A shot in which the ball travels diagonally across the net, from one sideline of the court to the other.

Deep shot A shot that bounces near the baseline (near the service line on a serve).

Default Failure to complete a scheduled match in a tournament; a defaulting player forfeits her or his position.

Deuce A score of 40-40 (the score is tied and each side has at least three points).

Deuce court The right-hand court is called the deuce court. The ball is served there on a deuce score.

Dink A ball returned so it floats across the net with extreme softness.

Double elimination A tournament in which a player or team must lose twice before being eliminated.

Double fault The failure of both service attempts to be good. It costs a point.

Doubles A game or match with four players, two on each team.

Down the line A shot hit parallel to the side line.

Draw The means of establishing who plays whom in a tournament.

Drive An offensive ball hit with force.

Drop shot A softly hit shot that barely travels over the net.

Drop volley A drop shot that is volleyed before it bounces.

Earned point A point won through skillful playing rather than through an opponent's mistake.

Eastern grip The forehand and backhand grips presented in this text as the standard basic forehand and backhand grips.

Error A point achieved through an obvious mistake rather than through skillful playing.

Face The hitting surface of the racket.

Fartleks A method of conditioning combining aerobic and anaerobic movement.

Fast court A court with a smooth surface, which causes the ball to bounce quick and low.

Fault A serve that fails to land in the proper serve square.

Feed-in The consolation bracket of a tournament in which a player who progresses further in the championship flight is placed upon losing into a corresponding round of the loser's bracket.

Fifteen The first point won by a player or team.

Flat shot A shot that travels in a straight line with little arc and little spin.

Floater A ball that moves slowly across the net in a high trajectory.

Foot fault Results from the server's stepping on the baseline, or into the playing court, before hitting the ball during the serve, or from a player's standing beyond the sideline or touching the wrong side of the center mark before the ball is served. Scored as a fault.

Forcing shot A ball hit with exceptional power and/or placement. A play in which, because of the speed and placement of the shot, the opponent is pulled out of position.

Forecourt The area between the net and the service line.

Forehand The stroke used to return balls hit to the right of a right-handed player or to the left of a left-handed player.

Forehand court For a right-handed player, the right-hand side of the court; for a left-handed player, the left-hand side of the court.

Forty The score when a player or team has won three points.

Frame The part of the racket that holds the strings.

Game That part of a set that is completed when one player or side wins four points, or wins two consecutive points after duece.

Graphite Expensive fibers used to produce extra-strength racket frames.

Grip The method of holding the racket handle. The term given the covering on the handle.

Groundstroke Forehand or backhand stroke made after the ball has bounced.

Gut Racket strings made from animal intestines.

Half volley Hitting the ball immediately after it bounces.

Handle The part of the racket that is gripped in the hand.

Head The part of the racket used to hit the ball; includes the frame and strings.

Hold serve To win a game in which one is the server.

Kevlar A synthetic fiber adding strength to racket frames.

Kill To smash the ball down hard.

Ladder tournament Players move on a verticle "ladder," up if they win, and down if they lose.

Let A point replayed because of interference. A serve that hits the top of the net but is otherwise good.

Linesperson In competition, a person responsible for calling balls that land outside the court.

Lob A ball hit high enough in the air to clear the net, usually by at least 10 feet, and intended to pass over the head of the net player.

Love Zero; no score.

Love game A game in which the winner never loses a point.

Love set A set in which the winner has won all games.

Match Singles or doubles play consisting of two out of three sets for all women's and most men's matches, or three out of five sets for many men's championship matches and tournaments.

Match point The game point that, if won, also will win the match for a player or team.

Midcourt The general area in the center of the playing court, midway between the net and baseline. Many balls bounce at the player's feet in this area; therefore, the player can be unusually vulnerable.

Midsize A racket head of approximately 85–100 square inches. Smaller than an oversize racket.

Mix up To vary the types of shots attempted.

Mixed doubles Male and female doubles partners constitute a team.

National Tennis Rating System A description of different tennis skills that helps the player to "self-place" himself or herself at the correct ability level.

Net game The play at net. Also called "net play."

Net person A player positioned at the net.

No ad Scoring system in which the winner is the first player or team to score four points.

Nylon A type of synthetic racket string.

Open face The angle of the hitting face of the racket when it is turned up, away from the court surface.

Opening A court position that allows an opponent a good chance to win the point.

Orthotics An artificial material that is inserted freely into footwear to add support to the arches of the feet and align the body more efficiently.

Out A ball landing outside the playing court.

Overhead smash *See* Smash.

Overside Refers to the largest of racket heads, which are 100 square inches or more. Larger than a midsize.

Overspin *See* Topspin.

Pace The speed or spin of a ball, which makes it bounce quickly.

Passing shot A ball hit out of reach of a net player.

Percentage tennis "Conservative" tennis that emphasizes cutting down on unnecessary errors and on errors at critical points.

Place To hit the ball to a desired area.

Placement A shot placed so accurately that an opponent cannot be expected to return it effectively.

Poach A doubles strategy in which the net player moves over to the partner's side of the court to make a volley.

Point Penalty System A penalty system designed to enforce fair play and good sportsmanship.

Power Holes Slits instead of holes on the racket frame through which the strings are inserted.

Pronation The outward rotation of the hand and wrist used when hitting a topspin serve. This wrist action allows the racket to move up and over the top of the ball. (Think of reaching overhead to unscrew a lightbulb in the ceiling.)

Rally Play in exclusion of the serve.

Retrieve A good return of a difficult shot.

Round-robin A tournament in which every player plays every other player.

Seed To arrange tournament matches so that top players don't play each other until the final rounds.

Semi-Western grip A forehand grip used by many players. The hand is turned on the racket handle from the Eastern forehand grip toward the right. This grip encourages extra topspin on the forehand.

Serve (service) Method of starting a point.

Service line The line that marks the base of the service court; parallel to the baseline and 21 feet from the net.

Set The part of a match that is completed when one player or side wins at least six games and is ahead by at least two games, or has won the tiebreaker.

Set point The game point that, if won, also will win the set for a player or team.

Sidespin A shot in which the ball spins to the side and bounces to the side. The sidespin slice is one of the most common types of serve.

Single elimination tournament A tournament in which a player is eliminated as soon as he or she loses.

Singles A match between two players.

Slice A backspin shot hit with the racket traveling down through the ball at less than a 45-degree angle with the court. *See also* Chip.

Slow court A court with a rough surface, which tends to make the ball bounce rather high and slow.

Smash A hard-hit overhead shot.

Spin Rotation of the ball caused by hitting it at an angle. *See* Topspin, Sidespin, Backspin.

Split The moment both feet land together and "split" apart, such as when approaching the net and the opponent is returning the ball.

Straight sets A match in which the winner has won all sets.

String tension Describes the tautness of the racket strings. Measured in pounds of weight.

Sudden death In no-ad scoring, when the score reaches 3-all.

Sweet spot The point of contact on the racket strings that best yields a solid hit.

Synthetic gut A racket "string" composed of several fibers of specially designed nylon.

Tape The fabric band that stretches across the top of the net. The lines of a clay court. Lead tape is a weighted tape that is applied to the head of a racket to make it heavier.

Tennis elbow A painful condition of the elbow joint commonly caused by hyperextension of the elbow or by excessive wrist action in tennis play.

Thirty The score when a player or team has won two points.

Throat The part of the racket between the handle and the head.

Tiebreaker When the score in any set reaches 6 games all, a twelve-point scoring system is used to determine the winner of the set. (A nine-point tiebreaker is also often used.)

Titanium A metal used to give rackets power, stiffness, and durability, thereby decreasing the weight needed in the racket frame itself.

Topspin Spin of the ball from top to bottom, caused by hitting up and through the ball. It makes the ball bounce fast and long and is used on most groundstrokes.

Trajectory The flight of the ball in relation to the top of the net.

Umpire The person who officiates matches.

Undercut A backspin caused by hitting down through the ball.

Underspin *See* Backspin, Slice, Chop.

Unseeded The players not favored to win or given any special place on draw in a tournament.

VASSS A no-ad, sudden death scoring system used extensively in the 1970s and 1980s. (No longer used in international competition.)

Volley To hit the ball before it bounces.

Wide-body A larger and thicker racket head that helps afford more power to lighter rackets.